Charles Dickens

A Very Peculiar History™

With no added gruel

'Unique of talents...'

Writer and historian Thomas Carlyle,
remembering Dickens in 1870

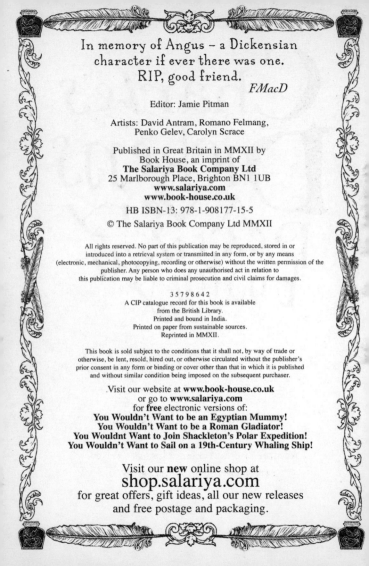

In memory of Angus – a Dickensian
character if ever there was one.
RIP, good friend.

FMacD

Editor: Jamie Pitman

Artists: David Antram, Romano Felmang,
Penko Gelev, Carolyn Scrace

Published in Great Britain in MMXII by
Book House, an imprint of
The Salariya Book Company Ltd
25 Marlborough Place, Brighton BN1 1UB
www.salariya.com
www.book-house.co.uk

HB ISBN-13: 978-1-908177-15-5

© The Salariya Book Company Ltd MMXII

3 5 7 9 8 6 4 2
A CIP catalogue record for this book is available
from the British Library.
Printed and bound in India.
Printed on paper from sustainable sources.
Reprinted in MMXII.

Visit our website at **www.book-house.co.uk**
or go to **www.salariya.com**
for **free** electronic versions of:
You Wouldn't Want to be an Egyptian Mummy!
You Wouldn't Want to be a Roman Gladiator!
You Wouldnt Want to Join Shackleton's Polar Expedition!
You Wouldn't Want to Sail on a 19th-Century Whaling Ship!

Visit our **new** online shop at
shop.salariya.com
for great offers, gift ideas, all our new releases
and free postage and packaging.

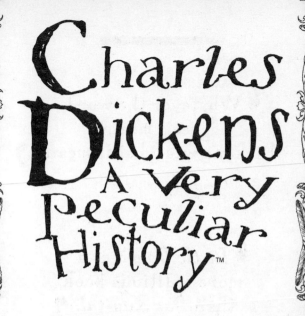

Charles Dickens
A Very Peculiar History™

With no added gruel

Written by
Fiona Macdonald

Created and designed by
David Salariya

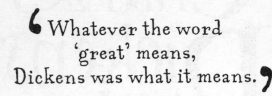

‘ Whatever the word
‘great’ means,
Dickens was what it means. ’

G. K. Chesterton, British writer, 1906

‘ *Little Dorrit* is a
more seditious book
than *Das Kapital*.’[1]

George Bernard Shaw, Irish writer, 1937

1. *Vastly influential work of economic and political analysis, published
in 1867 by Karl Marx, the founder of revolutionary Communism.*

Contents

Putting Dickens on the map

1. Charles Dickens is born in **Portsmouth, Hampshire** on 7 February 1812.

2. Dickens's family moves to **London** in 1822 when his father is transferred there.

3. Dickens marries Catherine Hogarth, who was born in **Edinburgh** in 1836. He is awarded the freedom of the city – a great honour – in 1841.

4. The whole Dickens family takes the first of many jolly summer holidays in **Broadstairs, Kent**, in 1837.

5. Dickens visits schools in north-east England in 1838. He is outraged by bad conditions – especially at **Bowes Hall, County Durham** – and features them in his next novel, *Nicholas Nickleby*.

6. Dickens's trip to **Yarmouth**, on the windswept Norfolk coast, in 1849, inspires many scenes in his semi-autobiographical novel *David Copperfield*.

7. Coketown, the industrial milltown in *Hard Times*, published in 1854, is partially based on 19th-century **Preston, Lancashire**.

8. In 1856, Dickens purchases Gad's Hill Place in **Higham, Kent**.

9. In **Manchester**, Dickens performs in a play opposite actress Ellen (Nelly) Ternan, and falls in love with her, 1857.

10. Dickens and Nelly narrowly escape death in a railway accident at **Staplehurst** in 1865.

‘ An amazing man... ’

Charles Dickens (about himself), 1849

WHY THE DICKENS?

Dickens was never modest. And why should he have been? Although born in obscure and relatively humble circumstances, he became far and away the most successful author of his age. By the time he died, relatively young (58), in 1870, he had become one of the two best-known writers in the English language – ever. The other was, of course, Shakespeare – by Dickens's time already enthroned as the English literary hero.

However, as Dickens knew very well, his own works were read, enjoyed – and understood – by many more people than Shakespeare's.[1] His readers came from all social backgrounds, and from all around the world.

A national treasure

And, while Shakespeare's works were admired, Dickens's were loved and treasured. As he himself declared, he aimed to become, through cheap, mass-produced editions of his books, 'a permanent inmate of many English homes'. And he succeeded. Although few families still have neat, matching sets of Dickens's novels on their shelves, almost everyone will have seen a version of at least one of his works at the cinema or on TV. All of Dickens's novels, even the last, unfinished, *The Mystery of Edwin Drood*, have been filmed at least once; many of them several times. The most popular is *Oliver Twist*.

---

1. *The same is still true today. A survey in 2011 named Dickens as Britain's favourite author. Peculiarly, it was conducted for a company selling spirits, although Dickens himself complained (in* Bleak House*) that 'Gin-drinking is the great vice of England.'*

Dickens's works have also inspired stage plays, musicals, most famously *Oliver!*, comic books and even a theme park ('Dickens World', at Chatham, Kent – once described in *The Guardian* newspaper as 'Disney gone to the dark side', and boasting a children's soft-play area called – yes, really – 'Fagin's Den'). Dickens's works have even been accused (if that is the right word) of inventing Christmas.

Happy Christmas?

Almost overnight, Dickens's short story *A Christmas Carol*, written in 1843 specially to cash in on publishers' peak sales season just before the annual Christmas holiday, created a powerful new 'tradition'. In many ways, it is still followed today. The 'Dickensian' Christmas became a season of exuberant, often excessive, consumption, as well as a time for sentiment, family reunion and once-a-year private charity. None of these, critics said, made adequate recompense for the exploitation of workers by employers, or the many other forms of social injustice that operated for the rest of the year in Victorian England.

Dickens had an amazing facility with words. At the peak of his powers he was writing at least two novels at once, together with many other shorter pieces. He also delighted in wordplay (think Sam Weller in *The Pickwick Papers*), in idiosyncratic ways of talking (from the gnomic 'Barkis is willin', to the downright sinister 'my dears' of Fagin), and in inventing extraordinary names for his characters. Many of these have found an enduring place in the English lexicon – almost all of us know what is meant by an 'artful dodger' or a 'scrooge'. And we know exactly what a man named 'Gradgrind' will be like.

Many of Dickens's phrases – from 'not to put too fine a point on it' to 'accidents will happen' – have also entered the international English-speaking consciousness. Even single words, used by Dickens, can have a powerful resonance. Try this test with your friends: if you shout out *'More!?'* in a tone of outrage mingled with surprise, what image comes into their minds?

A critical reception

It is only fair to add that, since Dickens died, his works have also attracted perhaps more than their fair share of parody or even ridicule. Today, BBC Radio's surreal *Bleak Expectations* attracts a devoted cult following, though few modern comments are perhaps so cruel as Oscar Wilde's clever put-down: 'One would have to have a heart of stone to read the death of Little Nell… without laughing.' But times change. When *The Old Curiosity Shop* (of which Nell is, of course, the tragic heroine) was reaching its conclusion, in 1841, over 6,000 people crowded onto the dockside in New York, desperate to read the final instalment. They shouted out to the sailors: 'Does Little Nell die?'

The baroque energy of Dickens's writing found a parallel in his own life story. Having despaired of his own future prospects aged 12, he seized his second chance when it came, worked incredibly hard, put the past firmly behind him and reinvented himself as a world-renowned celebrity. He fathered ten children (at least), had two parallel private lives, and met almost everyone worth knowing in mid-19th-century England – from Queen Victoria to Hans Christian Andersen. He loved amateur dramatics, practical jokes, seaside holidays, long walks, tidiness, 'bling' jewellery, horse-riding[1], pet dogs and garishly over-elaborate waistcoats. He made a fortune, but spent a lot of it helping his exceedingly feckless family. His favourite flower was the humble red geranium.

A tale of two centuries

In the year 2012, the world celebrates the 200th birthday of a man who could boast – with complete truthfulness – that his life and works had been 'amazing'. Thanks to years of patient scholarship and loving preservation, almost every detail of Dickens's life, and a very great many of the words he wrote, have been put on public display. So, if we ask (and it's extremely hard to avoid the temptation), '*WHAT* the Dickens?',[2] we can be fairly sure of finding an answer. However, in this little

---

1. On his orders, his favourite horse was shot when he died.
2. The phrase is originally from Shakespeare's The Merry Wives of Windsor, *act 3, scene 2.*

book, we shall also consider the rest of the 'famous five' journalistic queries: *Who* the Dickens? *Where? How? When?* And *Why?* Read on, and find out more.

You can't win them all...

'We do not believe in the permanence of his reputation... Our children will wonder what their ancestors could have meant by putting Dickens at the head of the novelists of his day.'

The Saturday Review, 1858

Tweet, tweet

No, not Dickens's pet raven – though that deserves a mention in itself[1] – but something much more modern. While he lived, Dickens was always keen to make use of the latest communications technology. Many of his novels first appeared in serial instalments in weekly or monthly newspapers and magazines. Their nearest modern equivalents are TV soaps, and they attracted every bit as much public interest and controversy. Dickens was also frequently photographed – there were over 200 images of him in circulation during his lifetime. He became one of the first authors to create an instantly recognisable celebrity public image.

If Dickens were alive today, we feel sure that he would also embrace all kinds of social media. So, from time to time throughout the book, we have included some of the great man's own words – as 'tweets'.

'Tweet'?

1. For several years, the raven, called 'Grip', was the terror of Dickens's children (it pecked fiercely at their ankles). After it died, Dickens had it stuffed and put on display.

Life and works

Charles Dickens's life was short – only 58 years – but full of incident, very busy, and sometimes hidden from public view. While he lived, Dickens tried to cover up unhappy or scandalous episodes in his childhood and later adult years. And, to make matters more confusing, he also 'borrowed' characters, events and sometimes whole storylines from his own life or from lives he had observed, and wove them into the plots of his novels. Sometimes, it can be difficult to separate Dickens fact from Dickens fiction.

However, for readers who would like an overview of Dickens's remarkable – and eventful – life history, we present a brief timeline on pages 166–186.

You can find another timeline, giving a summary of events, controversies, inventions and discoveries during Dickens's lifetime, on pages 114–119. These formed the background to – and interacted with – the main themes of many of his books.

'Some of the craftiest scoundrels that ever walked this earth... will gravely jot down in diaries the events of every day...'

Charles Dickens, *Nicholas Nickleby*, 1839

by
the
eing
He
ther
uch
ell as
h the

humbl...
with great disassociatio...

BIRTHS

On Friday, at Mile-end Terrace, the Lady of John Dickens, Esq., a son.

HAMPSHIRE COURIER – MONDAY, 10 FEBRUARY, 1812

393 Old Commercial Road (previously Mile End Terrace), Portsmouth. The birthplace of Charles John Huffam Dickens is now a museum dedicated to his life and works.

CHAPTER ONE

WHO THE DICKENS?

Dickens and family

T o begin, as they say, at the beginning. The first-ever time that Charles Dickens was mentioned in print was on 10 February 1812. That day, two little local newspapers, *The Hampshire Telegraph* and *The Hampshire Courier*, carried a simple personal announcement, recording the fact of his birth. However, like so much in the rest of Dickens's private life and public career, this seemingly straightforward text mingled fact with – if not exactly fiction, then a certain elasticity concerning the truth.

Stranger than fiction

Of course, every writer is influenced in some way or another by their upbringing and experiences. Of course, too, Dickens's novels are works of imagination in which his memories and observations are trimmed, stretched, re-shaped and, very often, distorted to serve the needs of entertainment, character and plot. However, Dickens's extended family – from his stern, story-telling grandmother to the sweet young actress who waited so patiently for him in a secret love-nest (in Slough!) – played a particularly powerful part in helping to shape his literary creations.

So, let us meet some of the people who shared their lives with Dickens. Who were they, and what were they like?

RealCDickens Charles Dickens

When I speak of home, I speak of the place where… those I love are gathered together. #nicknickle

173 years ago

Nearest and dearest

In his proud newspaper announcement, John Dickens, father of the new baby (his second child, and his first son), called himself 'Esquire'. This was the title given by members of polite British society to people they considered 'gentlemen': men of good breeding,[1] usually with a sufficient private income not to have to work for their living, except, perhaps, for managing a country estate. Just possibly, a gentleman might work to serve his country, becoming a priest in the Church of England or a commissioned officer in the Army or Navy.

John and Elizabeth Dickens rented their second house in a street advertising lodgings for 'superior naval persons'. That was how they liked to think of themselves!

1. a word that combined birth, upbringing, education, conduct and manners.

What's in a name?

John and Elizabeth Dickens followed strict tradition when naming their first-born son:

Charles – after the baby's grandfather, Elizabeth's father
John – after the baby's father
Huffam – after the baby's godfather, Christopher Huffam, a wealthy local businessman who supplied ships' rigging to the Navy.

Charles Dickens himself was much more imaginative when it came to choosing names for his own children (see pages 63–65).

'Below stairs'

But John Dickens was not gently born and bred. Instead – shameful secret! – he was the son of servants. His father had been steward[1] to the very rich, very grand Lord Crewe, and his widowed mother became the Crewe family's formidable housekeeper. Young Charles, her grandson, later remembered her as a great storyteller, who could keep adults

---

1. household manager.

and children happily entertained for hours at a time. Literary ability may not be inherited, but it can almost certainly be learned – or improved – by imitation. Dickens also learned how to tell a good (and funny) story from his father, who was well known for his witty anecdotes and genial conversation.

The Dickens grandparents were senior, trusted employees, but, even so, they were not acceptable members of polite society. However, young John Dickens learned 'genteel' manners and speech in the Crewes' upper-class surroundings; he was also fairly well educated there. By nature a 'lazy fellow' – or so his mother said – he grew up to be lively, impulsive, sociable, easy-going and hopeless at managing money. As an adult, he became stout, bald, over-dressed and rather pompous, but he was always somehow lovable, and good company.

In 1805, thanks again to Lord Crewe, young John Dickens was given a post in the government civil service, as a clerk in the Navy Pay Office. Surprisingly, considering his own chaotic finances, he did

rather well. He was honest, worked much harder than his mother had dared hope, and his colleagues and juniors liked his pleasant, cheery manner; he always seemed to have a joke to share. After winning promotion, and a higher salary, in 1809, young John got married.

That's no lady...

John Dickens's wife, or 'Lady' as he referred to her in the newspaper announcement, was Elizabeth Barrow, the sister of another Navy Pay Office clerk with promising career prospects. Surviving portraits show young Elizabeth (who was only 21 when she married, and 23 when baby Charles was born) as small, slim, dark-haired, bright-eyed, fashionably dressed and rather pretty. Witty and high-spirited,[1] she was also considerably tougher than her amiable husband. She had to be, to survive. She was also better educated, very fond of music and dancing, socially ambitious, and rather vain.

---

1. *Elizabeth's friends claimed that young Charles inherited 'a great deal of his genius (force of character and intelligence) from her'.*

Instant Dickens 1:
Sketches by Boz

What are they? A series of 56 short essays, 'illustrative of every-day life and every-day people' (Dickens). The essays are organised into four groups under the headings: 'Our Parish', 'Scenes', 'Characters' and 'Tales'. The first three groups are based on Dickens's own real-life observations; the last group is fiction.

When were they published? One by one, in different newspapers and magazines, between 1833 and 1837. They were later collected together and published in book form.

What is the plot or subject matter? They describe many different characters and the humorous or pathetic situations they find themselves in. Most of the 'sketches' are set in and around London.

How were they received? They were a great success.

Anything else? They were illustrated by top artist and cartoonist George Cruikshank.

And? Looking back, Dickens himself wrote in the 1840s: 'They comprise my first attempts at authorship. I am conscious of their often being extremely crude and ill-considered, and bearing obvious marks of haste and inexperience.'

fact and fiction 1

Later in life, Elizabeth Dickens liked to boast that she had been out dancing at a ball the night before Charles was born. But historians have investigated and found no evidence of any public dances (except perhaps a fairly small-scale gathering at the Beneficial Societies Hall) held on that night in the town (Portsmouth) where the Dickenses lived. A typical Dickens family story, perhaps?

What a disgrace!

Charming and sprightly though Elizabeth was, calling her his 'lady' (the female equivalent of 'esquire') was wishful thinking by her husband. However, Elizabeth did come from a higher-ranking background than his own. Her mother's family were respectable tradesmen, and her father, like her brother and her husband, worked for the Navy, but in an even more responsible position: he was Head of the Moneys Section.

The scandal was all the greater, therefore, when, just a few months after Elizabeth's wedding, it was found that her father had been systematically defrauding his employers for nine long years. The total sum stolen was massive, almost £6,000;[1] so was the disgrace. Elizabeth's father fled the country, leaving her brothers to support their mother and (if need be) their siblings. Two years later, while Elizabeth and her family had still not fully recovered from the shock, baby Charles Dickens was born.

More bills to pay

Worse was soon to come. John Dickens had never been careful with money; now, in 1812, after three years of marriage, he found his expenses had increased enormously. As well as a wife, he had two children and a nursemaid to support. Although his wife's widowed sister came to live with them, contributing her small pension to the family purse, there was never enough money to go around. Faced with alarming debts, he had to find somewhere

1. At the time Elizabeth married, Navy clerks, including her husband, earned around £100 per year.

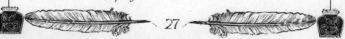

heaper to live. So, when baby Charles was barely six months old, the Dickens family made the first of many moves – leaving angry creditors (mostly tradesmen) behind them.

This restless habit of moving house stayed with Charles Dickens for the rest of his life. So did the notion – widespread in earlier centuries, though falling out of fashion by the time Dickens was born – that 'family' included more than just one married couple and their children. Aunts, uncles, grandparents, brothers-and-sisters-in-law, to say nothing of lodgers and servants, all played a part in Dickens's upbringing, and helped shape his future life.

RealCDickens Charles Dickens
Despair seldom comes with the first severe shock of misfortune.
#pickwick
175 years ago

RealCDickens Charles Dickens
'Poetry's unnat'ral; no man ever talked poetry…' #pickwick
175 years ago

Instant Dickens 2:
The Pickwick Papers

What is it/are they? A novel without a plot! A series of interlinked stories, featuring lovable, eccentric characters.

When were they published? In monthly instalments, from 1836 to 1837, and then as a single volume.

What was their plot or subject matter? Written as if by members of a 'corresponding society', who have promised to tell each other about their travels, adventures and mishaps. The stories are mostly good-hearted, and feature a duel, an elopement, a trip to the fashionable spa at Bath, comic servants, romantic misunderstandings, and a Christmas visit to an hospitable stately home.

How were they received? Slowly at first, but a new character (Cockney servant Sam Weller) and a new artist (Hablot 'Phiz' Browne), made them very popular. The final instalment sold 40,000 copies.

Anything else? *Pickwick* was originally planned by the publishers as a text to accompany pictures of country sports, but Dickens criticised the artist Robert Seymour's work. Stressed, short of money, anxious and with a history of mental ill-health, Seymour committed suicide.

fact and fiction 2

Looking back in 1845, Charles Dickens fondly remembered his father's good points:

'I knew my father to be as kind-hearted and generous a man as ever lived in the world. Everything that I can remember of his conduct to his wife, or children, or friends, in sickness or affliction, is beyond all praise. By me, as a sick child, he has watched day and night, unweariedly and patiently, many nights and days...'

Charles Dickens, autobiography notes given to John Forster, 1845/6

But he harshly satirised his worst fault – careless extravagance – by using him as the model for the bankrupt Mr Micawber in *David Copperfield*, 1849:

Mr Micawber knew well that:

'Annual income twenty pounds, annual expenditure nineteen nineteen six, result happiness. Annual income twenty pounds, annual expenditure twenty pounds ought and six, result misery.'

But, alas, Mr Micawber – like John Dickens – never followed his own good advice.

Dickens readily acknowledged his mother's early attempts to educate him:

> '...his [young Charles Dickens's] first desire
> for knowledge and his earliest passion for
> reading were awakened by his mother, from
> whom he learned the rudiments not only of
> English, but also a little later, of Latin.
> She taught him regularly every day for a
> long time, and taught him, he was
> convinced, thoroughly well...'

John Forster,
The Life of Charles Dickens, 1872–1876

But this gratitude did not stop Dickens mocking his mother's frivolous love of parties and relentless social climbing. He used her as the model for vain and silly Mrs Nickleby, in *Nicholas Nickleby*, 1838:

> '*We used to keep such hours! Twelve, one, two,
> three o'clock was nothing to us. Balls, dinner,
> card-parties – never were such rakes as the
> people about where we used to live. I often
> think now, I am sure, that however we could go
> through with it is quite astonishing – and that
> is just the evil of having a large connexion*[1]
> *and being a great deal sought after...*'

1. evil of having a large connection = the 'problem' of having so many
   friends and acquaintances. Mrs Nickleby is boasting, not
   complaining.

Happy days

In spite of frequent house-moves, and his parents' constant money worries, Charles Dickens looked back on his early childhood as a happy time, on the whole. The years his family spent at Chatham in Kent (when Charles was aged from five to ten) seemed full of easy, uncomplicated pleasures. He did not like the strict, joyless 'dame school' where he was sent once his mother finished teaching him, or the interminable hellfire sermons in the local chapel.

But everything else was wonderful: from barnstorming performances by rackety touring companies at the shabby local theatre, to lantern-slide shows in the darkened kitchen, parties and games with neighbours' children, long walks in country fields with his father, and exciting glimpses of sailing ships newly arrived from faraway lands. He loved playing with toy theatres, and wrote plays and songs for his cardboard actors. Best of all, he loved escaping into battered old books: tales of adventure, magic and fantasy, such as *Robinson Crusoe* and *Arabian Nights*, were his favourites.

At Chatham, young Charles could also observe a marvellous variety of people: soldiers, sailors, naval officers, foreign visitors, shipwrights, sail-makers, blacksmiths, chandlers, innkeepers, farmers – and respectable citizens and clergymen from the quiet, dusty (and very dull) cathedral city of Rochester nearby. There were huge cranes and other big machines to watch working at the dockyards – together with real, booming ships' cannon – and miserable prison-hulks, full of sinister, pathetic convicts, moored offshore.

'People-watching' remained a lifelong fascination – the curiouser, the better. Few of the characters in Dickens's novels were copied directly from life, but almost all were inspired by individuals he had seen or met, somewhere, at some time.

RealCDickens Charles Dickens
'We know, Mr. Weller – we, who are men of the world – that a good uniform must work its way with the women…' #pickwick
175 years ago

family matters

Like many other young nineteenth-century wives, Elizabeth Dickens spent the first years of her marriage almost perpetually pregnant. Charles was one of eight children – although two of his siblings, first Alfred, then Harriet, died in infancy.

John Dickens 1785/6–1851				Elizabeth Barrow 1789–1863			
Frances 1810–48	Charles 1812–70	Alfred d.1813	Letitia 1816–74	Harriet 1819–22	Frederick 1820–68	Alfred 1822–60	Augustus 1827–66

All through his childhood, Charles was very close to his older sister, Fanny. She was clever, musical, hard-working – and fun. Together, they went to a private school run by a kindly minister, William Giles; together they entertained visitors to the Dickens family home, and customers at the friendly local inn, where their father proudly displayed their talents. Fanny played the piano, while Charles performed comic 'action' songs. He was a good mimic, too.

After teaching music at London's Royal Academy of Music, Fanny married and moved away from the Dickens family. But when she collapsed (aged only 38, dangerously ill with tuberculosis) Charles brought her back to be near him.

Next to Fanny, Charles's younger brother Fred was his favourite. He took teenage Fred to live in his home in 1834. More than once, he helped Fred find work as a clerk. The brothers spoke nonsense-language to each other, and shared practical jokes, noisy, silly games and seaside holidays. Fred was cheerful and easy-going, like their father. And alas, like John Dickens, Fred was also hopeless at

fact and fiction 3

Dickens was moved – and shocked – by Fanny's calm acceptance of her approaching death, and she became the model for his most saintly heroines, in particular, Florence Dombey in *Dombey and Son*. Fanny's son Henry appears in Dickens stories as well, as tragic invalid Paul Dombey and as brave, frail Tiny Tim in *A Christmas Carol*.

handling money. He married – although everyone told him he could not afford to – and was soon deep in debt. He parted from his wife, was sent to prison, and became an alcoholic. He died aged 48; 'A wasted life', Charles lamented.

After John Dickens died, Charles humorously complained, 'I never had anything left to me but relations'. But, as well as caring for Fanny and Fred, he took his family responsibilities seriously:

- **1860** Brother Alfred Dickens dies; Charles helps support his family.

- **1862** Sister Letitia Dickens's husband dies. Charles arranges a pension for her.

- **1866** Brother Augustus Dickens dies, leaving two wives: one (deserted) in the UK; another (with children) in the USA. Charles gives money to them all.

Servants' scary stories

John Dickens and his family were poor, but they could always afford to hire at least one servant. Years later, Charles Dickens looked back to the effect that these household helpers had on the growth of his imagination. In particular, he describes how one nurse – probably Mary Weller – delighted in telling him ghoulish fairytales loosely based on the bloodthirsty 'Bluebeard' story: 'She had a fiendish enjoyment of my terrors.' Dickens also recalled how innocent children's toys, especially a jumping frog, a jack-in-the-box and, worst of all, a grinning paper mask, gave him horrifying nightmares.

Instant Dickens 3:
Oliver Twist

What is it? Dickens's second novel – and one of his most famous works.

When was it published? In monthly instalments from 1837 to 1839, and then as a single volume.

What is the plot or subject matter? The book tells the story of Oliver Twist, an orphan boy. He is sent to live in a workhouse (see page 115), where he is bullied by the adults in charge, and kept short of food. He escapes, but falls in with a gang of child criminals, masterminded by Fagin. He is rescued, reunited with his dead mother's family, and lives happily ever after.

How was it received? It was very, very popular, although Dickens was criticised for his sympathetic portrayal of criminals such as the 'Artful Dodger' and the prostitute, Nancy.

Anything else? Dickens was also criticised for choosing squalid 'low-life' London as a setting for his story.

And? The real-life London slum 'Jacob's Island', on which Dickens based his story, was soon afterwards cleared away.

'A terrible thing, Oliver... hangin'. The dawn... the noose, the gallows, the drop! You don't even have to be guilty, they'll hang you for anything these days, that's because they're so very fond of hangin'!'

Fagin in *Oliver Twist*

fact and fiction ⁋

Later critics have linked these childhood horrors – and Dickens's own fascinated memories of them as an adult – to perpetual themes in Dickens's writing:

'... its delight charged with terror ... and ... the terror charged with delight: its reality threatened by deception; its childhood ringed by mortality; its absurd, hilarious fancies proposed with gravity.'[1]

In some ways, the hectic, heightened atmosphere of Dickens's childhood dreams never left him, even in adult life.

first Love

In much the same way, Dickens's first, teenage love left a lasting impression on his later years – and on his writings. Biographers have suggested that this unhappy love affair, combined with his dislike of his mother, made him unable to trust women or relate to them in an emotionally satisfying manner for the rest of his life. Or was it simply the case, as

1. *Angus Wilson*, The World of Charles Dickens, *1970*.

Dickens's favourite daughter said, that: 'My father never understood women'?

Who was the girl – if we believe the biographers – who scarred young Dickens for life? Her name was Maria Beadnell, and – except, perhaps, to gratify her light-headed, light-hearted vanity – she had no real wish to harm him. She was petite and pretty, with dark curls and stylish clothes – and, like most young women of her era, it was her task to use her charms to catch the best possible husband. Her family expected it – and, being well off and deeply respectable, they would never have allowed her to marry Dickens anyway.

When Maria first met Dickens, in 1829 (he was 17), he was good-looking, energetic, witty and intelligent – but his job was humble, his earning power was low, and his family history of financial problems made him unsuitable husband material. For three years, Maria enjoyed flirting with him, but it was a dangerous game. He fell truly in love with her; but she did not share his feelings. Maria's parents sent her to France, out of harm's way. Dickens was (he said) left broken-hearted.

When Maria returned, prettier and more teasing than ever, it soon became clear that she no longer cared for Dickens. To her, she said, 'he was just a boy'. Dickens buttoned up his heart, hid his pain, and threw himself into his work. Tantalising young women like Maria feature in several of his later novels: the best example is Dora, in *David Copperfield*.

No going back

Over twenty years later, in 1855, Maria (by then married and with two daughters) wrote to Dickens, suggesting that they meet, for old times' sake. She warned Dickens that she was now 'toothless, fat, old and ugly', but he refused to accept the possibility, preferring to remember her as she once was, and to relive in his memory the pleasures of his first love. 'I have never been so happy a man since!' he declared.

RealCDickens Charles Dickens
Life is made of ever so many partings. #grtexp
151 years ago

But Maria was telling the truth, and, when they met, Dickens was horrified. Most unsuitably, Maria still behaved as if she were a silly, giggly girl – and, to make matters worse, she never stopped talking! After their first reunion, and the formal 'return-match' dinner party with her family, they hardly ever met again.

Soon afterwards, a ghastly female character called Flora Finching, very like a middle-aged Maria, appeared in the pages of Dickens's novel *Little Dorrit*. 'Spoiled and artless,' Dickens called her.

One wife, three sisters

When Dickens parted from Maria, aged 21, in 1833, he found that he greatly missed the happy, hospitable atmosphere of her home. He was, by now, immensely busy with work and amateur theatricals, but even so, Dickens felt rather lonely. He had no family home – or, indeed, any family able to help or shelter him. His lodgings were bleak and solitary; they lacked 'a woman's touch'.

It was therefore with great pleasure that Dickens accepted invitations from one of his employers, newspaper editor George Hogarth, to visit his house and meet his wife and children. It was here, with the Hogarths, one biographer has suggested, that Dickens quickly fell in love again – this time, with a kindly, cultured, contented middle-class family and their comfortable lifestyle.

'Amiable and excellent'[1]

Dickens chose Catherine, the oldest Hogarth daughter. She was neat and sweet, mild and gentle, plump and pleasant, good and true. She was decently educated, and far from stupid, but she did not – she could not – share Dickens's passion for words and ideas, or his love of vigorous sports and practical jokes, or his interest in social problems and politics. Her chief talent was needlework. Compared with Dickens, Catherine was conventional, unsophisticated – and maybe rather boring.

1. a statement Dickens made about Catherine.

So why did he marry? (They wed in 1836.) To comfort a broken heart, after parting with Maria? Because Catherine seemed so eager to please, and obviously admired him? Because Dickens wanted to feel again the joy of being in love – even if it was much less intense, now, second time around? Or was it because, like very many other 19th-century men, Dickens wanted a devoted wife to create a cosy home for him?

Certainly, at first, Dickens thought that he truly loved Catherine. He called her 'dearest Mouse' or 'darling Pig' and signed his letters with (literally) millions of kisses. But even before the wedding, there were perhaps signs of strains between them that did not bode well for the future. Catherine did not seem to understand that Dickens could not keep regular hours, or spare much free time for her. He must stay 'chained to his desk' (as he said) to finish assignments and meet deadlines. His writing work was much more than just a job; it was a whole way of living.

Instant Dickens 4: Nicholas Nickleby

What is it? Dickens's third novel. Comedy with a social conscience.

When was it published? In monthly instalments, 1838–1839.

What is the plot or subject matter? It is inspired by awful scenes Dickens and artist Hablot 'Phiz' Browne saw on a visit to schools in Yorkshire. Young, penniless Nicholas is sent to work at a boarding school where the boys are very badly treated. He leaves, taking a sickly pupil with him, and they have many adventures.

How was it received? An instant best-seller; the first instalment sold 50,000 copies.

Anything else? It was adapted for the stage even before the last instalments were published.

And? The book led to Dickens being awarded the Freedom of the city of Edinburgh – 'the first public recognition and encouragement I ever received', he said.

Newman Noggs
Lawyer's clerk

Fanny Squeers
Schoolmaster's
daughter

Mr Squeers
Sadistic
schoolmaster

reams are the bright creatures of poem and legend, who sport on earth in the night season, and melt away in the first beam of the sun, which lights grim care and stern reality on their daily pilgrimage through the world.

from *Nicholas Nickleby*

Not enough...

Dickens and Catherine honeymooned for just over a week alone, but never again spent time together without some friend or family member with them. It was soon clear that, by herself, Catherine simply could not give Dickens everything he wanted (he would have said 'needed'). While Dickens was clearly very happy to share Catherine's bed (their first child arrived nine months after the wedding, and nine more babies, plus at least two miscarriages followed in the next 16 years), from the very first days of their marriage, he sought lively conversation, new ideas, intelligent companionship, frivolous entertainment, poetic inspiration and even romance[1] from many other women.

RealCDickens Charles Dickens
Seeing her husband's face she leaned forward to give it a pat on the cheek, declaring it to be the best face in the world. #ourmutual
147 years ago

---

1. *technically 'innocent' but often alarmingly intense.*

'So perfect a creature'

Dickens's most passionate extra-marital friendship was with Mary Hogarth, his wife's younger sister. Mary came to stay with the newly married couple straight after the honeymoon, and made many visits to their home in the months afterwards. Young, carefree, slim, pretty and highly intelligent, Mary's 'delightful spirits' captivated Dickens. He was devastated when, in 1837, she collapsed and died in his arms, from undiagnosed heart disease. She was only 17; 'the grace and life of our home' had gone, he said. For the rest of his days, Dickens wore a ring he took from dead Mary's finger, and vowed that he would, at the end, be buried beside her.[1]

Mary's virtues filled Dickens's thoughts – 'She had not a fault'. And her lovely image haunted his dreams (he looked forward to this) – that is, until he told Catherine about them.

1. *This never happened.*

fact and fiction 5

Mary's friendship had offered Dickens something very special (and highly valued by countless 19th-century men): pure, innocent, almost spiritual love from an 'angel' devoted exclusively to their moral and practical well-being. Unlike Catherine, Mary was not 'tarnished' by physical love or distracted by the competing demands of motherhood. After Mary died, she remained forever unsullied and childlike. She never had to grow up.

Mary became the model for several heroines of Dickens's novels: especially Rose Maylie in *Oliver Twist*, and Little Nell in *The Old Curiosity Shop*.

Nell Trent, or 'Little Nell' as she is fondly known, is portrayed as innocent and angelic in *The Old Curiosity Shop*.

Catherine mourned her sister, too – but she could never compete, in Dickens's heart or mind, with such dead, untouchable perfection. Increasingly, Dickens complained about Catherine's dullness, undermined her confidence by rebuking her in public, criticised her untidiness – and told her that if she did not like his behaviour, he could always leave straight away. No wonder Catherine's sense of failure made her sulky, moody and depressed. At the same time, repeated pregnancies and postnatal problems ruined her figure, sapped her energy and weakened her health.

'I only want to be free'

Marital matters soon went from bad to worse. Catherine was shocked, but perhaps hardly surprised when, one day in 1857, she entered her bedroom and found workmen blocking up the doorway that led to Dickens's dressing room – and putting up a separate bed for him there. After 21 years, it was the end of their life together. Why end the marriage now? Why such a brutal gesture? Because, once again, Dickens was infatuated by a young,

Supernatural attraction!

Only rarely did Catherine protest at her husband's flirtations. But even her calm, placid temper was roused by the curious incident of the haunted banker's wife.

Dickens and Catherine met Augusta de la Rue (the elegant wife of a rich Swiss banker) while they were travelling in Italy. She claimed to be suffering from lurid, terrifying visions. Much to Catherine's displeasure, Dickens promised to cure her – by 'treating' her with newly fashionable hypnotism. Some years earlier, Dickens had studied mesmerism, a similar technique. Now, the quest to 'heal' Augusta, using his own mental powers, took up all his time and energy. Sometimes, he was so overwrought after a hypnotism session that he could not sleep, but paced round the bedroom all night long. Understandably, Catherine objected.

Years later, looking back, Dickens continued to protest that Catherine was being unreasonable about his experiments with hypnotism. After years of marriage to an extraordinary husband (Dickens!), surely she knew that sometimes he became obsessed with an idea or a project, and simply had to follow it through? Such intense concentration was – as Dickens might have said in modern language – 'all part of the package'. And, since it was a 'package' that let Catherine share in wealth, status and fancy foreign holidays, it might be better, Dickens suggested, if she just stayed quiet about it.

innocent girl. But this time, he wanted to do something more than sigh or dream about his feelings.

The girl who had won his heart was in some ways a surprising choice – she was not well-educated or well bred, and definitely not respectable. Her name was Ellen ('Nelly') Ternan, and she was an actress, a professional, hired to take one of the women's parts alongside male amateurs (Dickens and his friends) in public performances of Wilkie Collins's play *The Frozen Deep*. To Victorian moralists, an actress was little better than a prostitute; although Dickens's daughters enjoyed acting plays in private, like any other Victorian father, he would never allow them to appear on the public stage.

Nelly came from a long line of actors and actresses – and to Dickens, with his lifelong love of the theatre, that made her glamorous and fascinating. Young, charming, lively (she was only 18 when she met Dickens; he was 45), she still had an air of innocence. Surprisingly, Nelly was indeed a 'good girl' – although she and her sister had once been suspected by the police of prostitution (the notion was dismissed). So far, she had been able to rely on her good memory, clear voice, graceful figure, dancing skills, (moderate) acting talent and sheer hard work to earn a 'decent' living.

To the bedazzled Dickens, Nelly was like one of the pure, brave and long-suffering heroines of his novels – *Little Dorrit*, perhaps. Her youth and high spirits also reminded him of his dead sister-in-law Mary. And – even to the most dispassionate observer – she could hardly have been more different from dull, fat, boring, kindly, loyal, middle-aged Catherine.

RealCDickens Charles Dickens
Once a gentleman, and always a gentleman. #lildorrit
155 years ago

RealCDickens Charles Dickens
It is not easy to walk alone in the country without musing upon something. #lildorrit
155 years ago

Time to part

Unlike Dickens himself, Catherine – who still loved him – behaved with discretion and dignity in the months and years that followed. In 1858, she agreed to a separation;[1] Dickens found her a small but comfortable house, and paid her a (fairly) generous allowance every year, for life. So far, so tactful, but – of course! – the end of any celebrity's marriage (Dickens was by now very famous) led to a great deal of public gossip.

'Little housekeeper'

At first, the rumours centred on a third Hogarth sister, Georgina (one Glasgow newspaper confidently claimed that she had already had three children by Dickens). In fact, Georgina had been a hard-working part of the Dickens household since 1843. 'The best and truest friend a man ever had,' Dickens said. Georgina was brisk and busy where Catherine was slow, depressed and (Dickens said) lazy; full of energy and good sense, practical, well-organised, neat and tidy,

---

1. *Divorce was possible (just about), but deeply scandalous.*

55

strong and healthy, and very good at managing ten noisy, boisterous Dickens children. With Catherine, she made sure that there was always a welcome for Dickens's many visitors; she coped with countless house-moves and long family holidays (sometimes overseas). She organised the servants. The Dickens household could have been chaos without her. And, in spite of the way he treated her sister Catherine, in Georgina's eyes, Dickens could do no wrong. She never married, but devoted her whole life to serving Dickens.

A double life

Dickens was not in love with Georgina, though he liked and respected her. So did his children, who, he insisted, must stay with him; all obeyed, except Charley, the eldest, who took sides with his mother. Later, Dickens's favourite daughter, Katey, admitted that the coercion was unfair, but added that none of Dickens's children felt strong enough to defy their father. However, the rumours caused grave embarrassment to Georgina and the whole Hogarth family, and so, with the best of intentions, one of Dickens's male friends[1] tried to put a stop to them – by explaining the true situation to the gossips in a gentlemen's club. Dickens had not deserted Catherine for her sister, he said. No! He had left his devoted wife and fallen in love with an actress!

The news was dynamite, and the scandal rocked London. And, instead of keeping a dignified silence, Dickens fanned the flames by issuing a public statement, explaining and trying to justify his behaviour. Even today, Dickens's words seem in very questionable taste. He claimed that his wife was mad and a bad mother, that she wanted the separation, and that (in effect) only filthy-minded people (by which he meant Catherine's mother) would link the end of his marriage with his recent friendship with 'a virtuous and spotless' young lady, 'as innocent and pure … as my own dear daughters'.

> *'Nothing could surpass the misery*
> *and unhappiness of our home.'*
>
> Katey Dickens, aged 19,
> describing the year 1858

1. Novelist William Thackeray; it was many years before Dickens spoke to him again.

Instant Dickens 5:
The Old Curiosity Shop

What is it? A long, rather rambling novel; Dickens's fourth. A 'curiosity shop' is a junk shop or (more grandly) an antique shop.

When was it published? In weekly instalments, 1840–1841.

What is the plot or subject matter? Another 'campaigning' novel, this time concerned with the topics of extravagance, gambling and debt. Little Nell and her grandfather lose their home because of these, they flee a monstrous money lender, endure terrible hardships, then they both die.

How was it received? The long, tear-jerking death scenes were appreciated by Victorian readers.

Anything else? Dickens agonised for days before deciding whether or not to kill Little Nell. Eventually, he decided that the story would work best if she died. Afterwards, he said he missed her.

And? The book was published in weekly, not monthly, instalments. Dickens found this way of working absolutely exhausting.

Mr Chuckster
Lawyer's
dogsbody

**Dick
Swiveller**
Helpful
friend

Mr Harris
Puppeteer

**The
Marchioness**
Orphan servant

Sally Brass
'Dragon' wife

Sampson Brass
Unscrupulous
lawyer

Tom Codlin
Punch & Judy
man

Daniel Quilp
Evil
moneylender

Characters from *The Old Curiosity Shop*

faithful friend

In 1859, Nelly gave up the stage – and disappeared into the shadows of history. Dickens purchased houses for her, first in London, then in quiet suburban towns, where he visited her in secret, using a variety of assumed names. He also rented houses, where they both could live, in France. He introduced Nelly to his grown-up daughters and to Georgina. And – having most unfairly announced that he 'forgave' his wife Catherine (for what?) – Dickens admitted that he longed for her to die,[1] so that he could marry Nelly.

And Nelly? What of her? According to Dickens's daughter Katey, she was clever, and spent her time trying to educate herself so that she might be a fitting companion to Dickens. She also spent time visiting, or being visited by, her mother and her two sisters. But the constant need for secrecy must have been wearing; the days spent waiting for Dickens's visits must often have been lonely and – after

---

1. In fact, Catherine outlived Dickens by nine years. Shortly before her death, she asked that his early letters to her might be made public, so that 'people would know that he once loved me'.

the (probable) death of Dickens's (probable) baby – sometimes very sad.

After Dickens himself was dead, Nelly hid her past and married a deeply respectable clergyman schoolmaster. He never knew her secret; nor did their children, until long after she had died.

Ellen 'Nelly' Ternan (1839–1914)

'Why was I ever a father?'

Dickens loved babies. He played with them, laughed with them, gave them silly nicknames and – no doubt – pulled funny faces to amuse them. So he was delighted when his own first children were born – although less pleased when more, and more – and yet more – kept arriving. Rather unreasonably, he complained about his wife's repeated pregnancies. And, although Dickens's books celebrate close, happy, family values, Dickens found older children much less fun than infants, and much more difficult to manage. In a mixture of mock and genuine exasperation, he lamented, 'I have brought up the largest family… with the smallest disposition for doing anything for themselves.'

In some ways, that was a fair comment. Dickens's sons and daughters were all overshadowed by their famous father. They lacked his flair, drive and energy. Even so, he expected them to make their own way in the world through hard work and untiring effort, just as he had done. Compared with him, most were not terribly successful:

1837–1896 Charles Culliford[1] Boz (Charley)

Sent to Eton (Angela Burdett Coutts – see page 134 – paid); studied business in Germany, became a banker (but failed). Supported his mother when Dickens parted from her. Married daughter of publisher whom Dickens hated. Sub-editor on Dickens's magazine *All the Year Round*. Wrote *Dickens's Dictionary of London* and *Dickens's Dictionary of the Thames*.

1838–1896 Mary[2] (Mamie)

Unmarried; lived with Dickens until he died. Published biography of him.

1839–1929 Catherine Elizabeth Macready[3] (Katey)

Dickens's favourite. Studied art. Very unhappy at parents' separation; married sickly artist Charles Allston Collins to get away from family home. Widowed, then married artist Carlo Perugini.

1. *a name from Dickens's mother's family.*
2. *named after Dickens's dead sister-in-law, Mary Hogarth.*
3. *named after Dickens's actor friend, William Macready.*

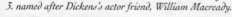

1841–1863 Walter Savage Landor[1]

Joined East India Company as junior officer in its private army. Died young, in India, leaving debts.

1844–1886 Francis Jeffrey[2] (Frank)

Went to India; joined mounted police. Returned to UK; inherited money, spent it. Went to Canada, became a 'Mountie'. Died in USA.

1845–1912 Alfred D'Orsay Tennyson[3]

Went to Australia. Late in life, returned to UK, gave public lectures about Dickens. Died on lecture tour in USA.

1847–1872 Sydney Smith Haldimand[4]

Joined Royal Navy; died young, after accident at sea. Left debts.

1. named in honour of English poet, Walter Savage Landor.
2. named after journalist friend of Dickens, Lord Francis Jeffrey, editor of The Edinburgh Review.
3. named after Poet Laureate Alfred, Lord Tennyson; and artist Alfred D'Orsay.
4. named after his two godfathers, William Haldimand and Henry Porter Smith, friends of the Dickens family.

1849–1933 Henry Fielding[1] (Harry)

Clever; won scholarship to Cambridge University. Studied law, became a judge, got knighthood ('Sir Henry'). Wrote books about Dickens, and gave readings from the novels.

1850–1851 Dora[2] Annie

A weak, sickly baby; had fits and died aged 8 months.

1852–1902 Edward Bulwer Lytton[3] (Plorn)

Emigrated to Australia, where he became a successful Australian MP. Never came back to UK.

> *'...though his children knew he was devotedly attached to them, there was still a kind of reserve on his part which seemed occasionally to come as a cloud between us and which I never quite understood.'*

> Sir Henry F. Dickens,
> *Memories of My Father*, 1928

---

1. *named after one of Dickens's favourite novelists, Henry Fielding.*
2. *named after Dora Spenlow, a character in* David Copperfield.
3. *named after Dickens's novelist friend, Edward Bulwer-Lytton, famed for opening a novel with 'It was a dark and stormy night...'.*

Instant Dickens 6:
Barnaby Rudge

What is it? One of only two historical novels written by Dickens. The other was *A Tale of Two Cities*.

When was it published? In weekly instalments, 1841

What is the plot or subject matter? Set in London during the anti-Catholic Gordon Riots of the 1780s, *Barnaby Rudge* is a love story with a disturbing background of mob violence, murder, madness and disorder.

How was it received? It was not so popular; Dickens was by now worried that readers might be getting tired of his writing.

Anything else? Dickens found the novel very hard to write; he roamed the streets of London looking for inspiration.

And? Among the cast of sinister characters, there is a pet raven – called 'Grip' – just like Dickens's own pet bird.

Father Time is not always a hard parent, and, though he tarries for none of his children, often lays his hand lightly upon those who have used him well; making them old men and women inexorably enough, but leaving their hearts and spirits young and in full vigour. With such people the grey head is but the impression of the old fellow's hand in giving them his blessing, and every wrinkle but a notch in the quiet calendar of a well-spent life.

from *Barnaby Rudge*

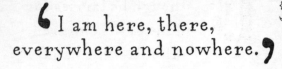

" I am here, there,
everywhere and nowhere. "

From a letter written
by Charles Dickens, 1867

" I can hardly expect you to
understand the restlessness
or waywardness of an
author's mind. "

From a letter written
by Charles Dickens, 1855

CHAPTER TWO

WHERE THE DICKENS?

At home and abroad

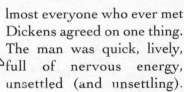

lmost everyone who ever met Dickens agreed on one thing. The man was quick, lively, full of nervous energy, unsettled (and unsettling). He was *restless*. He could never sit still (even his writing chair had little wheels on it). He wanted to be free.

Dickens would have agreed, as well. On the opposite page, you can read what he wrote about himself. On both occasions, he was making polite excuses to avoid meeting people; but, at the same time, he probably meant every word. The huge workload he chose to burden himself with, the stifling demands of his family life, plus the need to provide for a great many people, all made him, at times, desperately keen to escape. He wanted to be able to get right away from emotional, social – and contractual – pressures, to think, to recharge his batteries. And he often did so.

Letting off steam

When his writing was not going well, or when completing a dramatic chapter had drained him emotionally, Dickens liked to go for long, long walks or rides on horseback – all night if necessary. Sometimes, instead, he went rowing – exhausting himself by covering over 20 miles (32 kilometres) at a time. Without such violent exercise, Dickens said, he felt like an inflated, but tethered, balloon.

Kill or cure

Here's an excerpt from an urgent letter from Dickens to his friend:

> *'I am not well – and want a ride. Will you join me – say 2 o'Clock – for a hard trot of three hours?'*

Three hours' fast riding without a break would have been very tiring.

Getting the habit

It is often said that Dickens's restlessness stemmed from his early childhood experiences. Because of debts, his parents had had to move house a great many times, and even endure a spell in prison.

By the time Dickens was 12, he was not only working in the hated Warren's Blacking (sticky polish) Warehouse, but also lodging

alone, first with a ghastly family who 'watered the hash' (added water to the reheated minced meat they served boarders, to make it go further – ugh!), but then with a rather more kindly couple: 'immensely stout' and with 'an idiot son'. They became the model for the Garland family in *The Old Curiosity Shop* – but could never replace Dickens's own family.

By the time Dickens had reached 22 years of age, he had had enough of his family's constant changes of address and midnight 'flittings' to escape creditors. From now on, he would choose where he was going to live.

Onwards... and downwards

1812 Dickens family live in pleasant house in Mile End Terrace, Landport, Portsmouth.

1812 Debts increase. They move to smaller, cheaper house, Hawke Street, Portsmouth.

1813 Move to Southsea, Portsmouth.

1815 Move (for Navy work) to Norfolk Street, Marylebone, London.

1817 Move to Sheerness, then to Ordnance Terrace, Chatham (for Navy work – this means promotion and more pay).

1821 Debts. Move to smaller house (St Mary's Place) in poorer part of Chatham. Take lodger.

1822 Move (for Navy work – less pay) to 'wretched, squalid' Bayham Street, Camden Town, London.

fact and fiction 6

Later, Dickens used the Camden Town house – which came as a great shock to him (he was only 10) – as the model for the home of the poor but deserving Cratchit family, in *A Christmas Carol* (1843).

1823 Move (still with lodger) to Gower Street, central London. Debts increase.

1824 John Dickens is arrested for unpaid debts. Dickens family (except Charles and Fanny) live for months in Marshalsea Prison, London. Charles lodges in Little College Street, Camden Town, then in Lant Street, near the prison. Fanny is a boarder at the Royal Academy of Music in London.

Dickens family, including Charles, live first in Little College Street, then in Hampstead (still a suburban village). Fanny has to leave the Academy; there is no money for the fees.

Dickens family move to Johnson Street in the poor district of Somers Town, London.

1827–1831 Dickens family evicted from Johnson Street for not paying bills. They move to rented houses in Clarendon Square, Norfolk Street, George Street (all in London) and two different addresses in Hampstead.

1831 John Dickens bankrupt again. Dickens family at Margaret Street, Marylebone.

1832 Dickens family at Bentinck Street, Marylebone, London.

1834 John Dickens arrested for debt (again). Moves to North End, Holborn. Helped by a friend, Charles pays to set him free – and moves out of his parents' home for ever. He lives first of all in rooms in Buckingham Street, then in 'chambers' (small sets of rooms, for bachelors) at Furnival's Inn, close to St Paul's Cathedral.

> ❝We have a most extraordinary partiality for lounging about the streets. Whenever we have an hour to spare, there is nothing that we enjoy more than a little amateur vagrancy...❞

Dickens, in an article for the weekly magazine
Bell's Life in London, 1835.

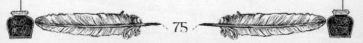

Instant Dickens 7:
Martin Chuzzlewit

What is it? A novel, the only one Dickens ever set (partly) in America.

When was it published? In monthly instalments, 1843–1844.

What is the plot or subject matter? Disowned by his grandfather, and disgusted by smug hypocrite Mr Pecksniff, Martin Chuzzlewit and a friend go to seek their fortunes in America. There is a sub-plot featuring a really nasty villain, Jonas, and two delightful young women, Cherry and Merry.

How was it received? British readers were lukewarm, whilst Americans were hostile and offended by Dickens's description of their frontier settlements.

Anything else? The book was dedicated to Angela Burdett Coutts, with whom Dickens was working to rescue 'fallen women' (see pages 134–135).

And? Drunken midwife Sairey Gamp – and her umbrella – make a welcome comic appearance. For almost 100 years, big black umbrellas were nicknamed 'gamps' after her.

Mr Pecksniff
Hypocrite

Sairey Gamp
Drunken
midwife

Mark Tapley
Servant

'Rich folks may ride on camels, but it an't so easy for 'em to see out of a needle's eye. That is my comfort, and I hope I knows it.'

Sarah 'Sairey' Gamp in *Martin Chuzzlewit*

Married life, family travels

In 1835, after Dickens became engaged to marry Catherine Hogarth, he took rooms in Brompton, south London, to be nearer to her. However, his plan did not work; he was often away, travelling as a roving reporter for London newspapers. When he and Catherine wed, they moved back to a larger set of chambers at Furnival's Inn – with a kitchen for servants in the basement – and then, in 1837 (after a brief stop-over in rented rooms), to a terraced house[1] in a smart, private development: Doughty Street.

Like many other Londoners – at least, those who could afford it – the Dickenses liked to escape the smelly, disease-ridden city during the summer months every year. In 1837, they rented a farmhouse in Hampstead and rooms in Calais, France. They also took the first of many summer holidays at Broadstairs, Charles's favourite seaside town. These summer excursions to the 'bracing' south coast of Britain, followed by many months further afield in France, Italy or Switzerland,

1. now the world-famour Dickens Museum.

funny peculiar

On seaside holidays, Dickens – who was unpredictable at the best of times – really liked to let his hair down. He played practical jokes and children's games on the beach, spoke nonsense language with his brother, alarmed complete strangers by stopping them in the street to tell them complicated jokes and puns, and pretended to fall in love with two most respectable maiden ladies, who were staying in a quiet boarding house to benefit from the sea air.

Sometimes, Dickens's 'fun' stopped being amusing and veered towards danger. Once, pretending to be overpowered by loving feelings, he picked a woman visitor up in his arms, carried her down the jetty, and, as the waves swirled round their knees, declared that they must both stay there until they drown. The woman was thoroughly frightened – and her best silk dress[1] was ruined (so were Dickens's shoes). Dickens's wife Catherine, who tried to stop the silly game (Dickens ignored her) was, understandably, very cross indeed.

Why did Dickens do it? For the thrill of shocking others, probably.

---

1. At that time, clothes were much more expensive than today.

set the pattern that Dickens and his family would follow for the next 20 years. Very often he invited London friends – fellow writers, artists, dramatists – to join them.

No place like home

After months away by the sea, or travelling to lakes, mountains and strange foreign cities, Dickens found that he needed the noise and bustle of London to provide a reassuring soundtrack while he worked – and the endlessly fascinating London crowd to intrigue and inspire him.

The opportunity – and anonymity – of London were endlessly exciting, and London itself was a character in several of Dickens's most popular works.

In *Sketches by Boz*, for example, written early in his career, Dickens practised his gift for seemingly light-hearted social commentary. In fact, his depictions of the London scene almost always have an agenda. Some, like his blow-by-blow account of a family outing to a tea-garden, or his 'diagnosis' of an outbreak of mad, extravagant new fashions in shop-front architecture and design, are simply, gently, satirical. They delight in the rich variety of human behaviour, and urge moderation, not excess. Others, like his account of stupid, self-seeking politicians, or shamelessly greedy eaters and drinkers at a charity dinner in aid of starving orphans, are much, much more savage.

The same mixture of curiosity, disgust – and delight – sent Dickens to visit prisons, hospitals, asylums, reform schools and burial grounds, along with theatres and concert halls, whenever he was abroad, in Europe and America. He was positively cheered after one visit to the Paris morgue. The strangeness of death exhilarated him. Also, of course, he was always on the lookout for powerful new themes and extraordinary details to include in his next novel. His works are famous for the strong sense of place they conjure up – from windswept East Anglia in *David Copperfield* to a sleepy cathedral city (based on childhood memories of Rochester) in *The Mystery of Edwin Drood*.

Boz on Slums

Most typical of all Dickens's descriptions of London are of the streets themselves. Here, he is complaining about – and celebrating – the 'rookeries' (city slums occupied by poor people) to the south of Oxford Street, right in the heart of the capital:

'The filthy and miserable appearance of this part of London can hardly be imagined by those... who have not witnessed it. Wretched houses with broken windows patched with rags and paper: every room let out to a different family, and in many instances to two or even three – fruit and 'sweet-stuff' manufacturers in the cellars, barbers and red-herring vendors in the front parlours, cobblers in the back; a bird-fancier in the first floor, three families on the second, starvation in the attics, Irishmen in the passage, a 'musician' in the front kitchen, and a charwoman[1] and five hungry children in the back one – filth everywhere – a gutter before the houses and a drain behind – clothes drying and slops emptying, from the windows; girls of fourteen or fifteen, with matted hair, walking about barefoot...; boys of all ages, in coats of all sizes and no coats at all; men and women, in every variety of scanty and dirty apparel, lounging, scolding, drinking, smoking, squabbling, fighting, and swearing...'

1. a woman employed to clean houses or offices.

As, on the ruined human wretch, vermin parasites appear, so these ruined shelters have bred a crowd of foul existence that crawls in and out of gaps in walls and boards.

Dickens's description of the slum, 'Tom-all-Alone's', in *Bleak House*

Instant Dickens 8: A Christmas Carol

What is it? A very short novel, written especially for the Christmas trade. Produced in attractive gift editions – which were too expensive for ordinary people to buy. Dickens lost a lot of money.

When was it published? 1843

What was the plot or subject matter? A miser, Ebenezer Scrooge, is persuaded by ghosts to 'enter into the Christmas spirit', and be kind to his workers and other poor people. His mean soul is contrasted with poor, sickly, but angelic Tiny Tim.

How was it received? Fellow novelist William Thackeray described the book as: 'to every man and woman who reads it, a personal kindness'.

Anything else? It helped to reinvent the 'traditional British Christmas' (see page 11) as a time of giving and goodwill. It was also said to have popularised the greeting 'Merry Christmas'.

And? It's now not so much a book as a national institution.

Ebenezer Scrooge
Miser

I have endeavoured in this Ghostly little book, to raise the Ghost of an Idea, which shall not put my readers out of humour with themselves, with each other, with the season, or with me.

from the introduction to
A Christmas Carol

Putting on the style

Having learned in boyhood to equate moving house with stress and poverty, in his adult life Dickens seemed determined to relocate to show the world just how much his circumstances had changed. Now, he moved from house to bigger, better house, in smart, wealthy districts of London – on the edge of fashionable Regent's Park; in select Tavistock Square. There were also practical reasons to move: Dickens always needed more space: to write, and to store his books and voluminous correspondence; or for entertaining writers, artists, thinkers, people fighting for good causes – all were proud to call him their friend. He needed nurseries, schoolrooms and playrooms for his fast-growing family, and attics, basements and back rooms for all the servants that his wife, daughters and sister-in-law found it necessary to employ.

Almost always, these smart new houses were rented; unlike today, few nineteenth-century people, apart from the very wealthy, owned property. Dickens did, however, purchase at least one very splendid house (Gad's Hill Place – see page 92). Almost always, as well, Dickens took a keen and very particular interest in their decoration and furnishing. He insisted on installing shower-baths (then a very new and daring invention) in all his homes – and on taking a bracing cold shower every day.

Sometimes, the women running Dickens's household – to say nothing of the workmen they employed – must have found this obsessive attention to detail more than a little bothersome. Certainly, his children hated his regular inspections of their bedrooms to check that they were tidy. If Dickens did not like what he saw – especially in his daughter's rooms (for him, neatness was a crucial virtue in a woman) – he would pin a note of complaint on their dressing tables.

RealCDickens Charles Dickens
In the little world in which children have their existence… there is nothing… so finely felt, as injustice.
#grtexp
151 years ago

America, America

In 1842, at the height of his new-found fame, Dickens, Catherine and her devoted maid-servant left their four children at home and sailed to spend several months touring the USA. Dickens wanted to see the proud, pioneering republic, which had won independence from Britain in 1776. He was fascinated by its promise of individual freedom, and by the idea of a wild, unexplored, 'frontier'.

The Dickenses met President John Tyler Jnr., saw big city sights, toured new schools and factories, and were warmly welcomed into many famous people's homes. They made steamboat trips down mighty rivers, crossed mountains in horse-drawn coaches, and visited virgin forests, settlers' log cabins and wide rolling prairies (where Catherine was afraid of Indian attack). They marvelled at the majesty of the Niagara Falls.

At a personal level, the tour was a great success:

'"Boz" was young, handsome, and possessed of wonderful genius, and everything relating to him and his family was of surpassing interest to them.'

The Atlantic Monthly, 1870

But Dickens was disgusted by the American habit of spitting tobacco – everywhere! – and appalled by the sight of black slavery. 'This is not the republic I came to see; this is not the republic of my imagination!' he declared. The same feelings were clear in his travel writings about America, and in the novel *Martin Chuzzlewit*, published in 1843–1844, soon after his return.

By the time Dickens returned to America for a final reading tour in 1867–1868, these earlier criticisms had been forgiven and forgotten (slavery had been abolished by then), and the American people welcomed him with the same generous enthusiasm as before. As Dickens himself remarked, the country had changed – and so had he. Although vast crowds flocked to hear his readings (and he tried to enjoy himself, meeting old friends, taking sleigh-rides in new York's snowy Central Park), the effort of long-distance travel, together with the strain of public performances, made him very unwell.

He completed the eastern seaboard tour (76 performances!), cancelled plans to travel further west, and, hardly able to eat, in great pain, and racked by 'the true American catarrh', headed for home. But he brought back with him what he went for – fees of over £20,000 (equivalent to more than £1,000,000 today).

A 'stupendous property'

In 1856, at the height of his fame, Dickens enjoyed creating his very own 'gentleman's residence' in the country. People with upper-class, old-style tastes called his alterations there 'suburban', but to Dickens, his final home was the undeniable sign that he had made a success of his career; that he had arrived.

Long ago, before he was 10 years old, Dickens had seen the house – it was called 'Gad's Hill Place' – as he went walking with his father in the countryside near Chatham. It was a well-known local landmark; the hill itself had famously featured in one of Shakespeare's plays.[1] With typically expansive – and (any onlooker would have said) unrealistic – optimism, John Dickens had told young Charles:

'If you lived to be very persevering, and were to work hard, you might some day come to live in it.'

---

1. in Henry IV, Part 1, when old reprobate Sir John Falstaff plans a highway robbery there.

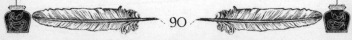

Charles never forgot his father's words and when, by chance, he learned that Gad's Hill Place was about to be sold, he was determined to purchase it. It became his home for the last 10 years of his life.

Gad's Hill Place's country situation also suited Dickens. It was isolated; a pack of fierce dogs – and a gardener with a gun! – kept curious intruders away. A specially built tunnel, passing under the road that ran through the grounds, allowed Dickens to wander safely, deep in thought, from one half of the garden to the other. A pretty, romantic Swiss chalet (a gift from an actor whose career he had promoted) became the ideal workroom, especially in summertime.

So near, so far

Sad to say, once Dickens had found his 'childhood dream' (Dickens's own words) home at Gad's Hill Place, he seemed fated to spend surprisingly little time there. He often had to travel to London, to meet publishers and artists, to check on the progress of his magazine *All the Year Round*, for meetings and

A summer retreat

Journalist Edmund Yates, a visitor to Gad's Hill Place, describes the daily routine Dickens set for his house guests:

'Delightful ... Breakfasted at nine, smoked ... cigar, read the paper, pottered about the garden ... All morning Dickens was at work ... luncheon at one ... [then the guests] assembled in the hall. Some walked, some drove, some simply pottered ... I elected to walk with Dickens ... the distance travelled was seldom less than 12 miles [19.3 kilometres], and the pace was good throughout...'

On summer afternoons, there might also be croquet or cricket on the lawns. In the evenings, Dickens liked music, dancing, and party games, such as charades.

Gad's Hill Place, Higham, Kent – Dickens's country home

dinners with powerful people trying to change the world, or to enjoy a visit to the theatre (still his great passion). He still rented a London flat for himself, and a house for his estranged wife, Catherine, together with homes for Nelly Ternan, first in Slough, then Peckham. He visited those incognito, as 'Mr Trigham'.

In 1858, Dickens began tours of Britain and America, giving public readings. He needed the money – not least to pay for all his different houses – but travelling and speaking kept him away from Gad's Hill Place for weeks at a time.

A final puzzle remains concerning Dickens's whereabouts upon his death. When he collapsed and died from a stroke in 1870, the world was told that this unhappy event had happened at Gad's Hill Place. But years later, rumours spread that Dickens had in fact been with Nelly Ternan when he was taken ill, and that he had been carried, secretly, while unconscious, back to his dream home to die.

Instant Dickens 9: four more Christmas tales

What are they? Four short books, also written specially for the Christmas market. Like *A Christmas Carol*, they were nicely bound and with beautiful illustrations.

When were they published? *The Chimes*, 1844; *The Cricket on the Hearth*, 1845; *The Battle of Life*, 1846; *The Haunted Man*, 1848

What was their plot or subject matter? All, except *The Battle of Life*, which is a love story, are fairytales, featuring ghosts, visions, spiritual lessons to be learned, social commentary – and happy endings. *The Chimes*, for example, campaigns powerfully for better treatment of the poor.

How were they received? The first two were extremely popular; the last two less so. But even 19th-century readers thought they were very sentimental.

Anything else? Described by Dickens as 'a whimsical sort of masque (entertainment) intended to awaken loving and forbearing thoughts'.

And? Soviet Communist leader Lenin famously walked out of a drama production of *The Cricket on the Hearth* in disgust at its sweet, gentle, Christian message.

'...there are not, I say, many people who
would care to sleep in a church.'

from the introduction to *The Chimes*, 1844

'It appeared as if there were a sort of match,
or trial of skill, you must understand,
between the kettle and the Cricket. And this
is what led to it, and how it came about.'

from *The Cricket on the Hearth*, 1845

'Once upon a time, it matters little when, and
in stalwart England, it matters little where,
a fierce battle was fought.'

Opening to *The Battle of Life*, 1846

'Everybody said so. Far be it from me to
assert that what everybody says must
be true. Everybody is, often, as likely to
be wrong as right.'

Opening to *The Haunted Man and
the Ghost's Bargain*, 1848

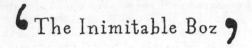

❛The Inimitable Boz❜

In 1836, after *The Pickwick Papers* first won
public fame for Dickens – though not yet a
fortune – William Giles, his kindly former
schoolmaster from Chatham, sent him a silver
snuff box, engraved with just the three
words above.

They touched Dickens to the heart –
and they were true. There was no-one else
quite like him.

CHAPTER THREE

WHAT THE DICKENS?

Meeting Mr Dickens

As the whole world knows, Boz, the clever, witty sketch-writer, the one-of-a-kind, grew and matured into a writer of novels that had the power to make readers laugh out loud or reach hurriedly for a pocket handkerchief to wipe away their tears. But how about Dickens the man? What was he like? How did he behave? How did he talk? What did he look like? What did he wear? And, if we could travel back in time to meet him, how well would we like him?

From his earliest years, Dickens's appearance always attracted comment. Let us, therefore, begin with external impressions, and then – if we dare – try to look beneath the surface.

As a child, Dickens was engaging and attractive. He was small and slight, but lively; by the time he reached eight years old, his teacher was already impressed by his 'bright appearance and unusual intelligence'. He wore his light brown hair (it darkened as he reached adulthood) cut just above shoulder-length, in curls. Unusually for a small boy, he liked to be neat and clean.

At junior school, Dickens wore uniform: long blue trousers, short jacket and white hat. At senior school, like his classmates, he wore a sailor suit and blue cap. Even then, he was 'very particular' about his clothes; by his later teenage years, he had developed his own personal – and rather unconventional – style. He caused comment by arriving for his first job, in a solicitor's office, wearing a military-style hat (complete with chinstrap) perched on one side of his head. Soon afterwards, he spent some of his first wages on a complete

new outfit. Unusually for the time, he was dressed head-to-toe in the same colour (dark brown): tight trousers, close-buttoned coat and tall hat. He also purchased a sweeping blue cloak, with velvet trimmings.

Later, as Dickens had more money to spend on clothes, his appearance became even more gaudy. He favoured flashy jewellery (rings and watch-chains), vivid, flower-patterned waistcoats, shiny patent-leather shoes (in daytime! on the beach!) and voluminous astrakhan[1] coats.

> *'Any man may be in good spirits and*
> *good temper if he is well-dressed.'*

Mark Tapley, in *Martin Chuzzlewit*, 1843

---

1. *Curled baby fleece. Traditionally, astrakhan was made from the skins of lambs that were less than three days old, or — worse still — had not yet been born (their mothers were killed and cut open). But Dickens probably did not know this.*

In trim

All his life Dickens remained slim and wiry, thanks to his love of strenuous exercise and very moderate eating habits. As an adult, he was around middling height – his American secretary called him 'a small, dapper fellow' – but he stood very upright, giving the impression that he was taller. He had a ruddy 'glowing' complexion (all that fresh air), yellowish teeth[1] and eyes that 'flashed like danger lamps' when he was angry or excited.

My way...

When young, Dickens liked to wear his naturally curly hair in fashionable ringlets ('effeminate!' thundered older men with less luxuriant locks), and kept it rather longer than was usual until he reached late middle age. As it thinned on top, he brushed strands across his head from the back and side. He cultivated a short 'imperial' beard and a long, neatly trimmed moustache.

1. In the USA, a tooth-powder company rather insultingly suggested, in its advertisements, that this was because he did not use the firm's products.

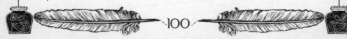

feed the mind?

- As a hungry child, at work, all Dickens could afford to eat was bread and milk for breakfast and – if he was lucky – rather dubious meat pies or slices of stale bread pudding (made with lard and dried fruit) for supper.

- As a young man, Dickens was fond of the favourite 'fast foods' of his day – boiled sausages and grilled chops, served piping hot and washed down with beer or wine. He also described buffet meals taken at inns while he was travelling: toast, cake, meat pie, cold beef, cold ham and fried eggs.

- As a generous host, Dickens gave lavish dinner parties (like his clothes, see below, these were sometimes criticised as 'too much'). His wife's cookery book – see pages 160-161 – preserves some of their household recipes. Dickens also liked to mix his own special gin punch to offer friends – the effects were said to be lethal!

- As he grew older, Dickens still fed his guests very well, but he himself ate simply – at least, by the standards of his day. He just had a snack of bread and cheese for lunch, and perhaps a glass of ale.

A cut above

Dickens's taste in hairdressing was not universally appreciated:

'[The] ... fashion he has of brushing his hair and goatee so resolutely forward gives him a comical Scotch-terrier look about the face...'

American writer Mark Twain, 1868

As flashy or even ridiculous as Dickens's clothes and hairstyles might have seemed to well-bred observers, almost everyone was impressed by his 'glowing and cordial' expression. His face seemed to radiate wit, intelligence, energy and – for most of the time – good humour. Even the stuffiest, most patronising people were ultimately charmed.

The master's voice

As might be expected from a man whose great love in life was amateur acting, Dickens had a clear, pleasant speaking voice, well able to express heights and depths of emotion – in anecdotes among friends (some of his after-dinner stories made them weep with laughter), as well as in public readings of his works, or when performing roles on stage.

fine and dandy

'He is a fine little fellow, Boz ... clear blue intelligent eyes, eyebrows that he arches amazingly, large, protrusive, rather loose mouth – a face of most extreme mobility... dresssed rather a la D'Orsay[1] than well...'

Historian and critic Thomas Carlyle, 1840

1. The Count D'Orsay was a famous – and scandalous – London dandy.

Instant Dickens 10:
Dombey and Son

What is it? A novel – the first that Dickens planned as a complete whole, rather than creating the plot as he wrote each fresh episode.

When was it published? In monthly instalments, 1846–1848.

What is the plot or subject matter? A rich merchant (Dombey) is desperate for a son to succeed him, but there are some things money can't buy. The book is fiercely critical of ruthless business people who don't value human qualities such as love and kindness.

How received? Readers cried – and purchased over 30,000 copies each month.

Anything else? There's another crowd-pleasing sentimental death bed scene; this time, young Paul Dombey dies.

And? Famous for an utterance by minor character Captain Cuttle: 'When found, make a note of.'

Mr Dombey
Miser

Mrs McStinger
Landlady

Captain Cuttle
Seafarer

Major Bagstock
'Tough and sly'

Characters from *Dombey and Son*

However, this dramatic talent also meant that Dickens was often able to hide his true feelings. Except when alone with his closest friends, he was probably always acting a part: dutiful family man, celebrity author, busy publisher, social campaigner… Unlike many other famous men of his day, Dickens had not absorbed – either at home or at an expensive, exclusive school – the formal rules of good behaviour or the self-assured manners of people born to privilege. Instead, he had to learn how to conduct himself in polite society – and he was constantly aware, as he said, that he had 'skeletons to hide'.

Dickens did not (at first) want people to know about his father's imprisonment for debt and his own early working life, or (later) about his relationship with Nelly Ternan. After moving to Gad's Hill Place, he made an enormous bonfire of old private papers. Who knows what gems of information have been lost?

The man behind the mask?

In 1840, Thomas Carlyle described Dickens as 'a quiet, shrewd-looking fellow, who seems to guess pretty well what he is, and what others are'. Very true! From early childhood, Dickens seems to have had a strong sense of his own 'special' identity. Looking back at his time in the blacking warehouse, for example, he expresses shock and dismay that a child with talents such as his own should have been reduced to such a miserable, menial existence.

This early trauma, together with his unreliable parents, failed first love, unfulfilling marriage and financial worries, left him emotionally guarded – and needy. It was a difficult combination. Later, observers commented that he developed 'portentous dignity and gravity'.[1] Amateur theatricals must have provided an escape – and instant gratification (he was a very good actor). So did the massive public approbation generated by his reading tours. Dickens loved company – and hated being alone.

1. *Mark Twain, 1870*

At a lighter level, Dickens was always happy to be the leader of any enjoyable jaunt, to take the chair at meetings, to be the public face of a good cause. Conversely, he was not a good 'team player' and disliked routinely deferring to others. Several of his friends were younger (he was generous with good advice); none dared compete. He had great confidence in his own opinions and his gifts as a writer. He laughed at his own jokes.

He was the life and soul of any party, persuading even the grandest or shyest guests to join in the dancing, play word and memory games, applaud his skill as a mimic, or marvel at his conjuring tricks. One perceptive critic has likened Dickens's love for neatness and order (in everything from his clothing to the arrangement of ornaments on his writing desk) to 'a thin crust over boiling imaginative chaos'.[1] Dickens himself said much the same thing about the extraordinary drive and energy he poured into his work, his daily routine, and his public persona: 'I should rust, break and die, if I spared myself. Much better to die doing.'

1. *Catherine Peters*, Charles Dickens, *1998.*

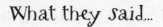

What they said...

'From one of our humblest authors, to one of our greatest.'

Queen Victoria, on sending Dickens a presentation copy of her own book: *Leaves from a Journal of our Life in the Highlands*, 1868

'Read [the] end of Charles Dickens's *American Notes* ... dreadful beyond words.'

Critic John Ruskin, 1874

'... what a jolly thing it is for a man to have written books like these books, and just filled people's hearts with pity.'

Novelist Robert Louis Stevenson, 1874

'About a year ago, from idle curiosity, I picked up *The Old Curiosity Shop*, ... rotten vulgar un-literary writing...'

Novelist Arnold Bennet 1898

'Is Dickens dead? Then will Father Christmas die, too?'

Reported remark from a little girl, name and date unknown.

Instant Dickens 11:
David Copperfield

What is it? A partly autobiographical novel –
Dickens's 'favourite child'.

When was it published? In monthly
instalments, 1849–1850.

What is the plot or subject matter? An orphan,
David Copperfield, is bullied by his stepfather
before being sent to work in a London factory.
He is poor and miserable. He makes friends
with the Micawber family, who are kindly but
always in debt. He is saved by eccentric aunt
Betsey Trotwood. Works as a lawyer's clerk,
marries child-bride Dora, becomes an author.
Dora dies, David remarries. The Micawbers
emigrate to Australia.

How was it received? Sales were slow at first,
but it soon became one of Dickens's most
popular works.

Anything else? This book was written in the
first person, and was based on Dickens's part-
finished autobiography, which his wife
(probably wisely) persuaded him not to publish.

And? As the president of the Dickens
Fellowship said, in 1932, to write *David
Copperfield*, Dickens 'dipped his quill into his
heart's blood.'

Daniel Peggotty
Fisherman

David Copperfield
Young man, later
author

Mr Murdstone
Wicked stepfather

Uriah Heep
Slimy lawyer's
clerk

Betsey Trotwood
Indomitable aunt

Mr Micawber
Debtor

Characters from *David Copperfield*

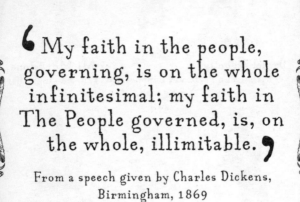

'My faith in the people, governing, is on the whole infinitesimal; my faith in The People governed, is, on the whole, illimitable.'

From a speech given by Charles Dickens, Birmingham, 1869

CHAPTER FOUR

WHEN THE DICKENS?

Dickens and his times

It is a truism to say that Dickens lived in changing times – when are times not changing? It is perhaps more useful to remember that Dickens lived at a time when writers, thinkers, politicians, engineers, factory-owners, newpaper editors – and their readers – were more than usually aware of the rapid pace of change. In front of their very eyes, Britain was being transformed from a largely rural and agricultural society into an urban and industrial one. On the whole, they considered that this was Progress, and good.

The best of times,
the worst of times

What was happening while Dickens was writing? (Rather a lot, actually...)

1812 Angry, skilled hand workers, nicknamed 'Luddites', riot and destroy new machines which they fear will do their work more quickly and cheaply and leave them unemployed.

1813 Jane Austen publishes *Pride and Prejudice*.

1813–1845 Elizabeth Fry campaigns for prison reform.

1815 Battle of Waterloo – Britain and its allies defeat Napoleon's France.

1817 Wild-child novelist Mary Shelley publishes *Frankenstein*.

1819 Peterloo Massacre: Peaceful protesters, meeting to listen to a radical speaker in Manchester, are charged by troops on horseback; many die.

1819–1824 Scandalous poet Lord Byron publishes *Don Juan*.

1820 Prince Regent becomes George IV.

1824 Combination Acts (that banned trade unions) repealed; union membership now legal.

1825 First public railway opens, from Stockton to Darlington (north-east England). Sir Marc Brunel builds first tunnel under the River Thames, London.

1829 Catholic Emancipation Act gives Roman Catholics in Britain equal civil rights with Protestants.
Home Secretary Robert Peel sets up the Metropolitan Police.
George Stephenson builds fast, reliable *Rocket* locomotive.
First horse-drawn buses in London.
Isambard Kingdom Brunel builds revolutionary suspension

bridge at Clifton, Bristol.

1830 William IV becomes king.

1831 Michael Faraday makes breakthrough experiments with electric current. Discovers electromagnetic induction.

1832 Parliament passes First Reform Act; voting system is made less corrupt; a limited number of men get the vote.

1833 Slavery abolished in British colonies (it has been illegal in Britain since 1772).

Factory Act bans children under 9 from full-time work.

1834 Tolpuddle Martyrs: six working men transported to Australia for joining a trade union.

Poor Law Amendment Act (also known as the New Poor Law) ends 'outdoor relief' (local payments) to poor. Sets up workhouses where poor people live and work in grim conditions in return for basic rations; they are hated and feared. Like many other people at that time, Dickens hopes that workhouses will solve the problem of poverty; sadly, hindsight proves him wrong.

1835 Municipal Corporations Act: local government is reformed. Town councils can now collect rates (local taxes) to pay for street lights, street cleaning and firefighters.

1835–1860 Houses of Parliament in London rebuilt in grand style.

1836 Charles Darwin completes voyage to southern hemisphere in HMS *Beagle*; gathers evidence that will later help him formulate theory of evolution (published 1859).

1837 Victoria becomes queen.

Isaac Pitman invents shorthand system of rapid writing.

1838 The People's Charter published in Birmingham: for the next 10 years, its supporters (known as Chartists) campaign for the right to vote for all adult men, annual parliaments, and secret ballots.

Instant Dickens 12:
Household Words and All the Year Round

What are they? Monthly magazines founded and edited (or 'conducted', as he liked to say) by Dickens.

When were they published? *Household Words*, 1850–1859; *All the Year Round*, 1859–1895

What was the plot or subject matter? To combine good-quality modern fiction (including much by Dickens, of course) with campaigning journalism that would improve and reform society.

How were they received? They were very popular; cheap, intelligent, approachable, easy to read. Sold between 40,000 and 100,000 copies per month.

Anything else? Dickens was a 'hands-on' editor. He himself said that the proofs he checked had so many lines and marks that they looked like inky fishing nets.

And? Dickens wrote Christmas stories for both magazines – trebling the sales!

First regular steamship service between England and USA, in Isambard Kingdom Brunel's *Great Western*.

Anti Corn-Law League founded; campaigns for cheaper bread prices, to feed poor working people.

1839 Riots by Chartists.

Photography publicly demonstrated by Fox Talbot (UK) and Daguerre (France).

Steam hammer (immensely powerful machine tool, used to make metal parts for tall buildings, ships and locomotives) invented by James Nasmyth.

1840 Penny Post service founded by government minister Rowland Hill.

1840–1870 'Railway Mania' – peak age of railway building in Britain.

1842 Mines Act bans women and children under 10 years old from working underground.

1843 Isambard Kingdom Brunel launches SS *Great Britain*, first steam-powered propeller-driven ocean-going liner.

William Wordsworth appointed Poet Laureate.

1844 Factory Act limits the number of hours per day that women and children are allowed to work.

Ragged Schools Union set up, funded by churches and charitable individuals. It aims to provide education for the very poor.

1845–1849 Potato Famine in Ireland; over a million people die, almost 8 million emigrate, many to the USA.

1846 Corn Laws repealed; price of grain no longer kept high to protect British farmers.

1847 Charlotte Brontë publishes *Jane Eyre*; Emily Brontë publishes *Wuthering Heights*.

Factory Act sets maximum working day at 10 hours for young people.

1848 'The Year of Revolutions': Socialist riots in many European cities.

Karl Marx publishes *The Communist Manifesto*.

Major outbreak of deadly cholera in London.

First Public Health Act aims to improve living conditions in towns by setting up local Boards of Health.

1850 For the first time, over half the British population lives in cities and towns.

Factory Act limits length of working week for women and young people to 60 hours.

Public Libraries Act encourages building of public reading rooms for all.

Alfred Tennyson becomes Poet Laureate.

1851 Great Exhibition in London displays British manufactured goods and other industrial achievements to the world.

1853 Elizabeth Gaskell publishes *Cranford*.

1854 Second cholera epidemic in London. John Snow discovers that the disease is spread by polluted drinking water.

Reform Schools set up in England and Wales to train young criminals for honest, useful work.

In France, Louis Pasteur discovers bacteria.

1854–1856 Britain fights Crimean War against Russia. Florence Nightingale nurses wounded soldiers.

1855 First cheap newspaper in London (*The Daily Telegraph*).

In Austria, Alfred Mendel discovers the laws of heredity.

1855–1875 Sir Joseph Bazalgette builds new underground sewerage system to improve public health in London.

1856 Police Act: there must be trained police offers in all regions of Britain.

Sir Henry Bessemer invents new method of mass-producing steel, using a hot-air blast furnace.

1857 The last prison-hulk (old ship, used as a dirty, unhealthy floating prison) destroyed by fire.

1858 'The Great Stink' in London caused by the polluted River Thames. The smell is so bad that Parliament cannot meet.

1860–1890 'The Scramble for Africa': Britain and other European nations compete to take over African lands.

1861–1865 Civil War in USA.

1863 First underground railway in London.
Slavery abolished in USA.

1864 International Red Cross humanitarian organisation founded.

1865 Joseph Lister discovers antiseptics; uses carbolic acid to kill bacteria.
The Salvation Army founded; it spreads the Christian message by providing help and welfare to poor people.
Lewis Carroll publishes *Alice's Adventures in Wonderland*.

1867 Second Reform Act. Voting rights extended to more working men.
London Society for Women's Suffrage set up to demand votes for women.
Transportation overseas is abolished as a punishment for criminals.

1868 Trades Union Congress founded.
Wilkie Collins (a great friend of Charles Dickens) publishes the first 'proper' detective story: *The Moonstone*.

1869 In Russia, Leo Tolstoy publishes *War and Peace*.

1870 Education Act. Local councils must provide elementary (primary) schools for all children.
Married Women's Property Act: wives can now keep their own earnings.

Instant Dickens 13:
Bleak House

What is it? A novel that marks a change in Dickens's writing. He now wants to make the world a better place, rather than chiefly to entertain readers.

When was it published? In monthly instalments, 1852–1853

What is the plot or subject matter? This book is an attack on the delays and corruption of the law, and on the hypocrisy that surrounded children born out of wedlock. There is a saintly heroine, Esther Summerson, a noblewoman with a shameful secret, a murder, a sinister lawyer – and a rag-and-bone merchant who dies of spontaneous combustion!

How was it received? It was a great success – but Dickens was exhausted.

Anything else? It features the first detective in English fiction, Inspector Bucket.

And? It also features a homeless, hopeless young crossing-sweeper, and London fog, everywhere.

Mr Chadband
Hypocritical clergyman

Inspector Bucket
Detective

Jo
Crossing sweeper

Mr Turveydrop
Dance teacher

Characters from *Bleak House*

A better future?

Throughout Dickens's lifetime, civil rights were being extended (rather grudgingly) by a small ruling elite to larger groups within society – although the majority of British people remained relatively poor and powerless long after Dickens's death in 1870.

What did Dickens think about the times he lived in? And how – if at all – did he reflect contemporary changes and controversies in his work?

Dickens admired Progress; he believed that it was the natural goal of all civilised societies. To stand in its way or to wish to turn the clock back to an imaginary golden age were both wrong. However, like many other thinking, feeling 19th-century men and women, Dickens was not content simply to admire the latest scientific and technical achievements. He criticised them, as well. And he strongly disapproved of the 'make money at all costs' ethos of many 19th-century entrepreneurs.

In fact, apart from in his northern factory-city novel *Hard Times*, scientific discoveries, new machines, booming overseas trade and fast-growing industries do not play a large part in his books. Nor do many other inventions developed during his lifetime, such as piped coal gas, which brought light to millions of houses, or the electric telegraph, which revolutionised communications, making it possible to send urgent signals vast distances, within minutes. Sometimes, 'inhuman' new inventions, such as railways, are unfavourably compared with older, more natural and humane, customs and practices.

Although many of Dickens's novels are written as if they were contemporary with his own adult lifetime, they are actually set in the generation just before – in the early years of the 19th century, when he was a boy. Perhaps that was part of their rather nostalgic charm for his readers.

A 'sentimental¹ radical'

- Did Dickens want to overthrow existing political and social institutions, and build a brave new world? No. He wanted 'improvement', through steady, gradual reform. His support for the poor and downtrodden sprang from sympathy, not ideology. But he hated snobbery, corruption, complacency, privilege and patronage – and was scornful of upper-class 'high society'.

- Did he support trade union marches, strikes and picketing, to demand better pay and working conditions for ordinary people? Generally, no. But Dickens did sympathise with direct action if poor workers' reasonable demands had been ignored, describing them as 'that unhappy class of society who find it so difficult to get a peaceful hearing'.

- Did he want rights for women (such as the vote, or the right to own property independently)? No. Although there were good schools for girls in London, he chose to have his daughters educated by old-fashioned private tutors, at home. And he thought women who had men to support them should stay at home, too. Their task was to create a loving, comfortable 'refuge' for their families.

1. In the mid 19th century, 'sentimental' meant 'full of feeling'; it was not an insult.

- **Did he worry about the way in which British Empire traders and soldiers treated overseas peoples?** No – he wrote that many non-Europeans were 'savages', who needed to be 'civilised'. However, as we have seen (page 89), he strongly opposed slavery.

- **Did he want better schools, cleaner cities, healthier houses, kinder prisons, better treatment for child labourers? Did he want more dedicated, less dishonest politicians, and a swifter, fairer system of justice for all?** Yes, of course. But he did not think that these failing institutions and wretched conditions were wrong in themselves; they just needed to be made to work better.

But 'Wait a minute!', we can hear some people say. Isn't Dickens famous for his campaigning journalism, and his support of good causes, public and private? his novels full of compassion for the weak and underprivileged? his call for the end of abuses of all kinds – from child abuse in boarding schools to procrastination and corruption in the law courts? Is he not shocked by the poverty, squalor, ignorance and sheer hopelessness of lives led in inner-city slums?

Yes, yes, yes and yes – of course he is. Dickens saw that there were many things wrong with British society – and said so, in his novels, and in letters, speeches and newspaper articles.

Novels with a cause

1838 *Oliver Twist* – child poverty and neglect, crime, slums, prostitution, the death penalty

1838–1839 *Nicholas Nickleby* – appalling schools, cruelty to children

1841 *The Old Curiosity Shop* – gambling, homelessness, poverty, child servants

1841 *Barnaby Rudge* – Political riots and disorder.

1843 *Martin Chuzzlewit* – Disillusionment with USA, hypocrisy, complacency

1843 *A Christmas Carol* – poverty, illness, unfair treatment of workers, the importance of personal charity

1846 *Dombey and Son* – avarice and ambition; childhood illness, unfair attitudes to daughters

1849 *David Copperfield* (Dickens's most autobiographical work) – children as workers, debt, poverty, imprisonment, the importance of personal charity, attitudes to mental illness

1852 *Bleak House* – illegitimacy, deceit, inheritance, the law's corruption and delays. Also, the danger of over-enthusiastic charity: seeking satisfaction from helping strangers (or foreigners), while neglecting local and family responsibilities

1854 *Hard Times* – ruthless, soulless industrial development, unprincipled politicians, the dangers of workers' unrest

1855 *Little Dorrit* – debt, imprisonment, charity, the power of a 'good woman'

1859 *A Tale of Two Cities* – the horrors of political violence (set in the French Revolution of 1789)

1860 *Great Expectations* – the gulf between social classes and between rich and poor, convicts and the treatment of prisoners, transportation, ill-gotten gains

1864 *Our Mutual Friend* – marriage for money, deceit and falsehood, blackmail, social climbers, the evils of wealth, fear of the workhouse

1870 *The Mystery of Edwin Drood* – orphans, murder, the London underworld, drugs

Which way forward?

But complaining was not enough. Dickens wanted the social ills he had diagnosed to be treated, or better still, cured. But how? Unlike many other social reformers of his day, Dickens was not a politician. He was invited, several times, to stand for election as a Member of Parliament, but always refused. One of his very first professional posts had been as a parliamentary reporter. The experience had left him with little respect for MPs as individuals, and not very much more for the institution as a whole.

When, in 1832, Parliament proposed laws giving (only a very limited number of) working men the vote, Dickens eagerly supported them. And he was scathing about rich, right-wing politicians[1] who called for a return to the 'Good Old Days' along with – as one well-known Victorian hymn put it: 'the rich man in his castle, the poor man at his gate'.[2] Dickens also disagreed with another popular Victorian sentiment: God might very

1. *The 'Young England' group within the Conservative Party.*
2. *Mrs C. F. Alexander, 'All Things Bright And Beautiful', 1848.*

Instant Dickens 14:
Hard Times

What is it? The second of Dickens's 'serious' novels about social problems, set in a northern industrial city, Coketown.

When was it published? In weekly instalments, 1854

What is the plot or subject matter? Thomas Gradgrind is a practical man; he wants facts, nothing else. He does not know how to love his children; as a result, the children both get into serious trouble...

How was it received? It sold well, but was controversial. Some critics thought that it was 'sullen socialism'; others said that Dickens was right to make people feel guilty about living in a very unequal society.

Anything else? *Hard Times* was based on a real strike among starving cotton-workers in Lancashire. It was Dickens's first and only northern book.

And? Writing the book was extremely difficult; 'I am three parts mad', Dickens said.

I believe...

Dickens writes to his teenage son, who is about to leave home and emigrate to Australia:

'I have always been anxious not to weary my children with [religious observances] before they are old enough to form opinions respecting them. You will therefore understand the better that I now most solemnly impress upon you the truth and beauty of the Christian religion, as it came from Christ Himself, and the impossibility of your going far wrong if you humbly but heartily respect it...

Never abandon the wholesome practice of saying your own private prayers, night and morning. I have never abandoned it myself, and I know the comfort of it.'

Letter from Charles Dickens to his youngest son, Plorn (Edward), 1868

RealCDickens Charles Dickens
Ask no questions, and you'll be told no lies. #grtexp
151 years ago

RealCDickens Charles Dickens
Take nothing on its looks; take everything on evidence. There's no better rule. #grtexp
151 years ago

well be 'in His heaven', but all was not 'right with the world'.[1] In his private life, Dickens was a sincere, although low-key Christian (see page opposite), but he kept his religious views very much to himself.

Words not deeds?

However, compared with many other progressive writers, thinkers and campaigners, Dickens's views were moderate and cautious. He was, after all, a member of the well-meaning, liberal-minded, comfortably-off middle class. He admired hard work, thrift, determination, self-sacrifice, self-control and self-improvement.

That word 'self' is very revealing. Ultimately, Dickens believed that society could only be reformed by sustained individual efforts to be better. As he said in 1869 (see page 112), he had little faith in parliaments (or the ruling class), but enormous respect for people. He put his faith in the power of 'human decency' to change the world. He wanted moral reform, not political revolution: 'Our business is to use life well.'

1. from Robert Browning's poem, 'Pippa Passes', 1841.

Happy ever after?

To many people, Dickens's moral approach to social reform was hopelessly optimistic – and limited. As Dickens knew very well (the critics argued) crime, drunkenness, violence, despair and many other social problems were caused by ignorance and poverty. Unless there was greater equality – of wealth, power, education and opportunity – things would never get better. In the light of this, the happy endings[1] pictured in many of Dickens's stories were (in modern language) a 'cop-out'.

> '[In Dickens's novels] … Really, there is no objective [aim in life] except to marry the heroine, settle down, live solvently and be kind. And you can do that much better in private life.'
>
> George Orwell, 1937

---

1. Boy gets girl, they have a large family, they are provided with money and/or a house by some amazing stroke of luck, no-one has to work or grapple with big public problems.

Instant Dickens 15:
Little Dorrit

What is it? Another 'social issues' novel. Some say Dickens's best.

When was it published? In monthly instalments, 1857–1858

What is the plot or subject matter? The book is a fierce attack on government bureaucracy, and the corruption that money can bring to family and social ties. Father Dorrit is in prison for debt; Amy ('Little') Dorrit is small and weak but saintly. She has a foolish but glamorous older sister, and a wild brother. Father Dorrit inherits a fortune; the family becomes mean and proud, except for Little Dorrit. She nurses and helps a family friend (whom she secretly loves) when he goes to prison...

How was it received? Attacked by many, who disliked Dickens's portrayal of official laziness and corruption, and thought the book 'gloomy'. It sold well, regardless.

Anything else? This was the most profitable of all Dickens's works during his lifetime.

And? Another book based on Dickens's childhood memories of prison. It was originally called 'Nobody's Fault'.

Cosy Cottage?

As well as writing and campaigning, Dickens often took practial action to help less fortunate members of society. He gave readings of his work for charity, attended countless fundraising gatherings, found jobs for and gave money to several friends in need (as well as his demanding family) and, for many years, worked closely with heiress Angela Burdett Coutts (1814–1906) helping to organise numerous charitable projects.

The wealthiest woman in Britain, Burdett Coutts spent her life giving her whole fortune to good causes. Founder, among many, many other things, of schools, churches, soup kitchens, a couple of bishoprics, the National Society for the Prevention of Cruelty to Children, the British Beekeepers' Association – and a friend of Florence Nightingale – she was also rumoured to have had the courage to propose marriage to great, formidable national hero, the widowed Duke of Wellington (he refused).

But back to Dickens; with Miss Burdett Coutts, from 1836 to 1843, he planned and organised the 'Urania Cottage' experiment. The 'cottage' was a large house in Lime Grove, then on the outskirts of London. On Dickens's orders, it was converted for use as a refuge for homeless, destitute women, including ex-prisoners and prostitutes. Once 'rescued' and safely installed there, they were nursed back to health and strength, trained in useful skills such as reading and sewing, then transported, mostly to Australia, to start a new life in a new land, where their past would either not be known, or could hopefully be forgotten, even by themselves.

Dickens took a great personal interest in all aspects of Urania Cottage. He looked for – and found – the building, complete with a pleasant garden. He helped choose the staff, the furnishings – including a piano, the epitome of respectable, womanly, domestic entertainment – and even the women's 'uniforms' (Dickens thought these should be 'colourful'). He interviewed prospective inmates and privately helped several of those who did not win – or want – admission. He wrote 'An Appeal to Fallen Women', and arranged for it to be circulated to prisons, to attract more applicants.

'She is degraded and fallen, but not lost, having the shelter … the means of Return to Happiness … are now about to be put into her own hands…'

Dickens looks forward to a bright new future for an inmate of Urania Cottage.

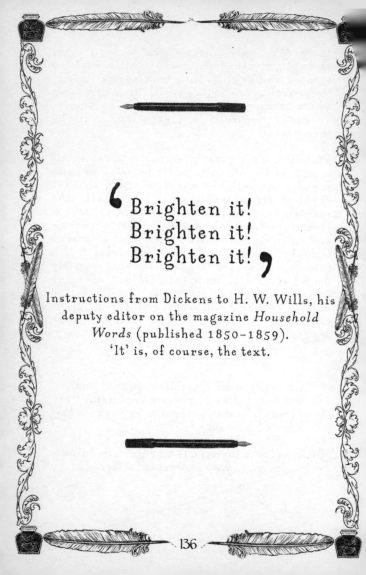

‘ Brighten it!
Brighten it!
Brighten it! ’

Instructions from Dickens to H. W. Wills, his
deputy editor on the magazine *Household
Words* (published 1850–1859).
'It' is, of course, the text.

CHAPTER FIVE

HOW THE DICKENS?

Writing and publishing

I n 1906, writer G. K. Chesterton had the audacity to remark: 'Dickens is a great writer even if he is not a good writer.' What (the Dickens!) did such a double-edged compliment mean? Was Chesterton commenting on the novels that Dickens wrote, or on his prodigious non-fiction output as a journalist? Was he criticising Dickens's writing style, or praising his plots and characters? Was Chesterton referring to Dickens's use of his writing skills – and name and fame – in support of good causes? Or was he just describing his worldwide celebrity status, and his remarkable popularity?

Any – or all – of these aspects of Dickens's work might have prompted Chesterton's rather acid comment. And he was not alone. Here's novelist E. M. Forster, no slouch himself at telling an intriguing tale, in 1927: 'Those who dislike Dickens have an excellent case. He ought to be bad…'

Forster thought that Dickens failed to create rounded characters in his books, but relied instead on 'types and caricatures': exaggerated, two-dimensional stereotypes, with no inner life for readers to care about or believe in. Others criticised Dickens for the amazing coincidences that help his characters escape from death and danger, and for the incredible twists and turns of fate that lead them to improbably happy endings.

Some people find Dickens's texts too long, his language too elaborate, his humour heavy-handed and his descriptions self-conscious and showy. But even E. M. Forster had to admit that, against all rules and expectations, Dickens managed in his books to create 'a vision of humanity' that was sympathetic and profound.

Good, bad or indifferent, even Dickens's sternest critics admit that he was a very powerful writer. In 1846, novelist William Thackeray rushed into the offices of *Punch*,[1] waving the latest instalment of *Dombey and Son*, and saying, 'There, read that! … against such power as this no-one has a chance … it is unsurpassed – it is stupendous!'

So, why did Dickens's books create such excitement in the past, and why do they still have such an impact today? Why have his stories been turned into plays, movies (about 200 so far, and counting), cartoons, musicals and goodness knows how many other formats? Why is his text, his 'voice', so instantly recognisable? Why, in spite of his often sordid subject matter, did he become a much-loved national treasure – and an international superstar? How the Dickens did he do it?

RealCDickens Charles Dickens
Don't leave off hoping, or it's of no use doing anything. Hope, hope, to the last! #nicknickle
173 years ago

1. a famous satirical magzine.

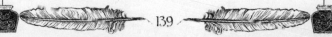

Instant Dickens 16:
A *Tale of Two Cities*

What is it? Dickens's second, and most successful, historical novel. It's based on Thomas Carlyle's *The French Revolution: A History* of 1837.

When was it published? In weekly instalments, 1859

What is the plot or subject matter? Set during the French Revolution of 1789, and the years that followed. The 'two cities' are Paris and London. Dickens contrasts arrogant old French aristocracy with idealistic but bloodthirsty revolutionaries. There is a love story, a case of heroic mistaken identity, and some bravura passages of descriptive writing.

How was it received? It was very popular.

Anything else? The plot features the guillotine and a body snatcher. How gruesome! The heroine is a portrait of Nelly Ternan.

And? *A Tale of Two Cities* is the best-selling novel of all time, anywhere. Around 200 million copies have been sold.

It was the best of times, it was the worst of times, it was the age of wisdom, it was the age of foolishness, it was the epoch of belief, it was the epoch of incredulity, it was the season of Light, it was the season of Darkness, it was the spring of hope, it was the winter of despair...

from *A Tale of Two Cities*

Step by step

Dickens never intended to be an author; he originally hoped to be an actor (see page 172). But a combination of circumstances and opportunities turned him into a professional writer, almost before he knew it. As Dickens himself said:

'I presume most writers of fiction write, partly from their imagination; and partly from their experience. I have had recourse to both sources.'

- Dickens's parents were good storytellers; fluent, witty and charming. Dickens's mother had ambition; his father had the optimism – though not the self-discipline – needed for a freelance career.

- From a very early age, Dickens's parents, household servants and teachers encouraged him to read, and told him lurid, exciting stories. They took him to theatres and music halls. All food for his imagination!

- Dickens was a skilful mimic and a talented actor. He loved drama, magic and mystery. He had great powers of observation, and a natural curiosity about people and places.

- As a reporter in law courts and Parliament, then as a solictor's clerk, Dickens learned to listen carefully to how people spoke – as well as to what they said – and to pay close attention to details. As a newspaper journalist, he had to write quickly and to length, and meet tight deadlines.

Between them, all these jobs gave Dickens the chance to experiment with many different ways of writing: dry, dusty documents, dramatic descriptions, imaginative flights of fancy, light-hearted sketches and letters, and passionate, persuasive arguments.

RealCDickens Charles Dickens
skewered through and through with office-pens, and bound hand and foot with red tape #dcopper
162 years ago

How to write like Dickens

- Get up at 7 am every day – no slacking! Have a cold shower, then dress as smartly as you can.

- At 8 am, have a sustaining but moderate breakfast: usually eggs, ham, toast.

- Get to your study by 9 am.

- Make sure your desk is neat and tidy, and that any ornaments there – such as your favourite little china statue of a monkey – are carefully arranged in order.

- Pull up your favourite chair. It's a typical 19th-century design; dark polished wood, with decorative turned legs, ornately carved back panels, and arms that curve round in a semicircle. And it's on wheels!

- Always have a good supply of goose-feather quill pens, blue ink, and small (around 7 in x 8 in [18 cm x 20 cm]) sheets of pale grey paper ready to hand.

- Make sure that the whole house is silent. Bangs, crashes, shrieks and any sudden noise disturb you and spoil your concentration. Your children and servants have learned to tiptoe.

- Write hard and fast. When busy with a novel or a newspaper article, you aim to complete around 2,000 words every day. But other days you will be correcting proofs, editing junior authors' work, or writing letters (over 14,000 of these survive – goodness knows how many you wrote altogether).

- By 2 pm, you're ready for a break – ideally some violent exercise. Ride a horse, go for a very long country walk or roam around the streets of London.

- By around 5 pm, you've worked up an appetite. Have a hot snack at an inn, or a meal with friends, or go home to eat dinner with your family.

- In the evening, there will be more reading and perhaps writing to do, but try to find time to play with your children, or listen to music, or go to the theatre, or invite friends to visit.

- Work six days a week if you can, but always give yourself a day off on Sundays.

RealCDickens Charles Dickens

The healthy air of morning fell like breath from angels, on the sleeping town #oldcshop

171 years ago

Taking the plunge

In 1833, for the very first time, Dickens submitted a sample of his creative writing to a publisher (the *Monthly Magazine*). He posted it 'stealthily, one evening at twilight, with fear and trembling, into a dark letter-box, up a dark court in Fleet Street.' Dickens need not have worried; his piece was a great success. After that, the satisfaction of a job well done – and of winning praise, and (eventually) earning very good money – drove him on and on…

Man at Work

'*I was lying on the sofa endeavouring to keep perfectly quiet, while my father wrote busily and rapidly at his desk, when he suddenly jumped up from his chair and rushed to a mirror which hung near, and in which I could see the reflection of some extraordinary facial contortions he was making…*'

Dickens's daughter, Mamie.[1]

1. *After that, she says, Dickens then began talking rapidly – to himself – in a low voice, 'acting out' the scene he was writing.*

Rich and rare, weird and wonderful

Dickens's delight in language – its rich range of meanings, its strange and wonderful sounds – is clearly displayed throughout his work. The opening lines of his novels, for example, are some of the most arresting ever created:

'Marley was dead…'
A Christmas Carol

'Now, what I want is facts…'
Hard Times

'Night is generally my time for walking…'
The Old Curiosity Shop

'Whether I shall turn out to be the hero of my own life, or whether that station will be held by anybody else, these pages must show…'
David Copperfield

Dickens also had wonderful fun with the names he gave the characters in his novels (there were 989 of them when the experts last made a list[1]). Although they often sound spontaneous, Dickens gave careful thought to each one, drawing up lists of possibilities before making a final decision.

- Some are gentle and playful: Rosa Bud, the Cheeryble Brothers, Tiny Tim...

- Some are humorous or mocking: self-important Serjeant Buzfuz, do-gooding Mrs Jellaby, Edmund Sparkler (who is always proposing marriage), fanatical bird-fancier Paul Sweedlepipe, careless young Toots...

- Others are rather more sinister, evoking threat, misery or danger by association, or simply through their sounds: Smike, Gradgrind, Magwitch, Slyme, Dodson and Fogg (crooked lawyers), and Josiah Bounderby, the banker.

1. *John R. Greenfield*, Dictionary of British Literary Characters, *1994.*

Let me entertain you...

But all Dickens's early experiences, and all his fun with words and names, would have been useless to him as a professional writer if he had not been able to publish his books, or attract readers to them. Dickens was not a 'literary' novelist, who wrote to please himself, explore new styles and forms, or to demonstrate the latest theories. First and foremost, he was an entertainer. He gave readers what they enjoyed, what they wanted – and what they could afford. Then, once he had caught their attention, he could, if he chose, ask them to think about more important issues.

How did Dickens manage this? By adapting his way of working and his writing style to the new media of his day: cheap, mass-produced, weekly or monthly magazines. These had become popular after new, inexpensive ways of printing text and illustrations had been invented around 1858, and after less costly – but coarser – paper, machine-made, or made from woodpulp rather than recycled rags, first became available around 1820–1860.

Instant Dickens 17:
Great Expectations

What is it? A novel, partly autobiographical. Written in the first person, like *David Copperfield*.

When was it published? In weekly instalments, 1860–1861.

What is the plot or subject matter? Pip, a child from a humble family, is sent to meet the eccentric spinster Miss Havisham; he falls in love with Estella, a cruel, tormenting girl. He is suddenly told he is rich but the money eventually proves to be from surly escaped convict Magwitch. Pip loses his money and learns to appreciate his old friends. Estella has also learned her lesson. They agree to part – will they really?

How was it received? It was hailed as a masterpiece.

Anything else? The book was very successful in America, France, Australia and many other countries.

And? Originally, the story had a less happy ending, but a novelist friend persuaded Dickens to change it.

With some vague misgiving that she might get upon the table then and there and die at once, the complete realisation of the ghastly waxwork at the Fair, I shrank under her touch.

Pip walks with Miss Havisham
in *Great Expectations*

Almost all Dickens's novels were first published in instalments, and only later, once the whole story was complete, bound into books. Writing this way was very hard work for Dickens – he had to meet printers' deadlines every week or month – but it it also gave his stories freshness. And it gave him plenty of scope for exciting 'cliffhangers' at the end of each instalment – a good way of making sure that readers purchased the next issue of his magazine.

Writing in this revolutionary, 'serial' way made Dickens's stories surprisingly modern. They were interactive. He could play down unpopular characters or create new storylines in an instant response to public opinion. The cheapness of each instalment – plus the fact that each was read aloud to groups of eager listeners – created a whole new mass market for fiction.

Dickens was sensitive to criticism from these readers – and genuinely encouraged by their praise. He hoped, also, that the popularity of his works would improve the pay and status of professional authors.

Into print – Dickens and the publishing business

1836 Leaves staff of *Morning Chronicle* to write full time. *Sketches by Boz* collected from many different papers and magazines and published in book form by John Macrone. After publication, Dickens buys back their copyright. Meets John Forster, a journalist who becomes Dickens's friend, advisor, editor, proofreader and biographer.

1836–1837 Publishers Chapman and Hall ask Dickens to write sketches: *The Pickwick Papers*. Chapman and Hall publish them in instalments from 1836 to 1837, then in book form in 1839.

1837–1841 John Macrone dies. Dickens contributes to anthology *Pic Nic Tales*; all profits go to help Macrone's widow and children.

1837 Dickens becomes editor of magazine, *Bentley's Miscellany* (owner and publisher Richard Bentley). *Oliver Twist* is published in instalments in the *Miscellany*.

1838 *Oliver Twist* published in book form by Bentley. *Nicholas Nickleby* published in instalments in the *Miscellany*.

1839 Dickens resigns from *Bentley's Miscellany*. Quarrels with Bentley over copyright of *Oliver Twist*. Chapman and Hall publish *Nicholas Nickleby* in book form and all Dickens's subsequent novels (as books) from 1840 to 1844 and from 1858 to 1870.

1840–1841 Dickens publishes weekly story magazine, *Master Humphrey's Clock*. It contains instalments of his next two novels, *The Old Curiosity Shop* and *Barnaby Rudge*.

1842 Copyright Act passed in the UK. Strengthens authors' rights to claim copyright in their works, and receive

payment for copies. Unlicensed foreign copying made illegal.

1842 Dickens travels to USA and Canada. Is angered that his writings are not protected by copyright laws there – though American publishers do pay for advance page-proofs. Calls for reform of US copyright laws; this causes offence. Breaks off all connection with his US publishers, Lea and Blanchard.

1843 Dickens attempts to form a Society of Authors, to advise, support and guide professional writers. Dickens complains bitterly that Chapman and Hall are not advertising his books, especially his latest, *A Christmas Carol*.

1844 Quarrels with Chapman and Hall; he wants more money. Signs deal with rival UK publishers: Bradbury and Evans.

1846 Becomes editor of newspaper *The Daily News* (but only for two months; the job does not leave him time for writing).

1847 Plans revolutionary new 'Cheap Editions' of his novels.

1848 Signs deal with US publishers Harpers, even though (he alleges) they illegally 'pirated' some of his works earlier.

1850 Dickens launches new weekly magazine, *Household Words*, published by Bradbury and Evans. Dickens is editor as well as one of the chief contributors (he calls himself the 'Conductor'). He has a sub-editor, William Henry Wills, to help him, but, in the nine years of its publication, the magazine contains contributions from 390 different authors, together with advertisements. It's a major feat of organisation to run it, while also writing novels.

1851 Acts in play (written by his friend, novelist Edward Bulwer-Lytton) in aid of the Guild of Literature and Art, a charity that helps writers and artists.

1851 First public readings (from *A Christmas Carol*, for charity, no fee). These public readings soon prove to be excellent

'Working the copyrights'

As a young writer, Dickens sold the rights to publish his work very cheaply – and felt that he had been unfairly treated. His sense of injustice led at first to quarrels with publishers, and then to plans to make as much money from each book as possible. He persuaded publishers to issue each novel in several different formats, to appeal to the widest range of buyers. There was a handsome 'Library Edition', a solid 'People's Edition' and an affordable 'Cheap Edition'; there was also a special 'Charles Dickens Edition' – plus the original weekly or monthly instalments of each novel, issued in paper covers in magazines.

publicity and very profitable. They also increase the sales of Dickens's novels and magazines.

1858 First paid public readings from his novels, in London. First provincial reading tour, to many parts of Britain.

1858–1859 Dickens separates from his wife, and issues a statement. It appears in *Household Words*. He also sends it to *Punch*, another Bradbury and Evans magazine. They refuse to publish it. Furious, Dickens tries to buy *Household Words*, but Bradbury and Evans won't sell their share (one quarter). Dickens takes them to court, wins, pays them off, and closes *Household Words* down.

Dickens parts permanently with Bradbury and Evans. His later novels are all published in book form by Chapman and Hall.

1859 Starts new magazine, *All the Year Round*, to replace *Household Words*. Dickens is in total control: owner, publisher, editor and a major contributor. His four last novels first appear in instalments there. This new venture is an instant success:

'So well has All the Year Round *gone that it was yesterday able to repay me, with five per cent interest, all the money I advanced for its establishment (paper, print etc. all paid, down to the last number), and yet to leave a good £500 [1] balance at the banker's!'*

Dickens, quoted in John Forster,
The Life of Charles Dickens, 1872–1876

1859 Second provincial reading tour.
1861 Dickens's son Charley marries Bessie Evans, daughter of the publisher; Dickens refuses to go to the wedding.
Third provincial reading tour.
1862 Discusses possible reading tour of Australia.
Dickens ends quarrel with Charley; appoints him sub-editor of *All the Year Round*.
1866 Fourth provincial reading tour; also holds very popular readings in London.
1867–1868 Massively successful and exhausting reading tour of the USA.
1868 Farewell reading tour of Britain begins.
1869 Farewell reading tour continues, but performances after 15 March are cancelled.
1870 Dickens leaves *All the Year Round* to Charley in his will. It continues publication until 1895.

1. *£37,500 in today's money*

❛ I hold my inventive capacity
on the stern condition that
it must master my whole
life, often have complete
possession of me, make its
own demands on me... ❜

Charles Dickens, 1855

Instant Dickens 18:
Our Mutual friend

What is it? Dickens's last complete novel. Dark and depressed; it features no comedy.

When was it published? In monthly instalments, 1864–1865.

What is the plot or subject matter? Inheritance, fraud, trickery, attempted murder and disguise. Love corrupted by greed. Love between people of different rank. London, its river, and the haunted, criminal slums beside it, are main 'characters' in the story.

How was it received? Fair to middling. Reading tours boosted book sales.

Anything else? When the story was almost complete, the manuscript was nearly lost in the Staplehurst train crash of 1865; Dickens and Nelly Ternan were (scandalously) travelling together. Dickens had to return later to their wrecked carriage, in order to retrieve it.

And? For this book, Dickens chose a new illustrator, Marcus Stone; his pictures were grim and realistic, not light-hearted and entertaining.

Rogue Riderhood
Blackmailer

Silas Wegg
Rascal, street trader

It was a foggy day in London, and the fog was heavy and dark. Animate London, with smarting eyes and irritated lungs, was blinking, wheezing, and choking; inanimate London was a sooty spectre, divided in purpose between being visible and invisible, and so being wholly neither.

from *Our Mutual Friend*

A taste of Dickens

In the mid-19th century, just like today, cookery books were very popular. And so no-one was surprised when, in 1851, a volume with the catchy title: *What Shall We Have for Dinner?* achieved considerable success. It was reprinted several times over the next 10 years before changing food fashions caused its popularity to wither.

According to the title page, the author was one 'Lady Maria Clutterbuck'. But there was no such person. She was a character in a play that members of the Dickens family performed at the home of wealthy friends: the part of Lady Maria was taken by Dickens's wife, Catherine.

The Dickens family now had not one, but two, authors under its roof (it was later to have five; after Dickens's death, his daughter Mamie wrote a rather one-sided account of her father's life and edited a collection of his letters; his sons Charley and Henry were also authors).

Catherine Dickens was not normally in the habit of asserting herself in public, so why, with Britain's most famous novelist for a husband, did she write too? Probably for the money. After all, Catherine did have plenty of experience in providing meals for a large family and many friends. Her menus are sensible and practical; she likes simple dishes and seasonal ingredients, and some of her recipes –

especially those for fish – seem to be based on favourites from her Scottish childhood.

Some Dickens enthusiasts have claimed that Charles, not Catherine, wrote the book, but experts think this is unlikely. However, he probably helped Catherine plan and edit it, or at least discussed its detailed contents with her. And, almost certainly, he wrote the introduction.

To serve 20–30 people, Catherine Dickens suggested:

First course

Cold Salmon, Asparagus Soup, Fried Fish

Main course

Shoulder of Lamb, Chicken in Sauce

Vegetable

New Potatoes, Peas

Savoury

Lobster Patties

Dessert

Almond Liqueur Jelly, Ice Pudding.

A few
^ Last words...

Charles Dickens died, ill and exhausted, on 9 June 1870. According to his daughter Mamie, he had spent the whole of his last day working feverishly on his final novel, *The Mystery of Edwin Drood*. Whether this was true or not (see page 93), it sounds as if it ought to have been. Dickens was nothing if not hardworking, however great the effort required. As he himself said, in a letter, in 1847:

'The world is not a dream, but a reality, of which we are the chief part, and in which we must be up and doing something.'

In his will, Dickens asked to be buried in Rochester Cathedral, close to his house at Gad's Hill Place and to Chatham, his childhood home – and also the subject of several beautiful, almost mystical, passages in *The Mystery of Edwin Drood*. But his devoted public thought otherwise; Westminster Abbey in London, the resting place of kings and heroes, would surely be more appropriate! The campaign was led by *The Times* newspaper, in typically thunderous form:

'Statesmen, men of science, philanthropists, the acknowledged benefactors of their race, might pass away, and yet not leave the void which will be caused by the death of Charles Dickens.'

The Times, 1870

The quiet and private funeral took place on 14 June; Dickens was buried at the Abbey, in Poets' Corner, between dramatist Richard Sheridan (died 1816) and composer George Frederick Handel (died 1759). It took two whole days for all the people who wished to pay their last respects to file past his grave.

Even if Dickens had not always succeeded, like his alter-ego David Copperfield, as 'the hero of my own life', he ended his days as a loved and respected national icon. After death, he achived even more, becoming part of the cultural landscape throughout the English-speaking world:

'Whether you approve of him or not, he is there, like the Nelson Column.'

George Orwell, 1937

Instant Dickens 19:
The Mystery of Edwin Drood

What is it? The novel that Dickens left unfinished when he died. A new type of 'sensation' novel – less plot, more atmosphere.

When was it published? In monthly instalments, 1870. Only six out of twelve were completed.

What was the plot or subject matter? Edwin Drood's and Rosa Bud's fathers have promised them in marriage to each other. They are friends but not in love. What should they do? They become involved in a tangle of intrigue and murder, obsession and addiction, secrecy and decay.

How was it received? Readers were delighted; the first instalment sold 50,000.

Anything else? Dickens visited opium dens by the docks in London to research the details of his story.

And? It contains some of Dickens's finest descriptive writing.

Why was this? Just what was the Dickens magic? Long before Dickens's death, one reviwer had suggested an answer:

> *Every reader will tell you that he has made acquaintance with [Dickens characters] ... and that he shall never forget them as long as he lives. There lies the greatest triumph a novelist can have...*

Blackwood's Edinburgh Magazine, 1858

In 1842, on Dickens's first tour of America, his railway carriage was mobbed by fans. Seeing the crowd, a market woman asked a fellow stall-holder, 'What's the matter?'

> *'Why,' said the man, 'it's Dickens. They've got him in here!'*
> *'Well, what has he been doing?' said she.*
> *'He ain't been doing nothing,' answered the man. 'He writes books.'*
> *'O,' said the woman, indignantly, 'is that all?'*

Atlantic Monthly, 1870.

'FULLNESS OF LIFE & ENERGY'
A Charles Dickens chronology

1812 Charles Dickens (CD) born at Mile End Terrace, Landport (now part of Portsmouth, Hampshire) on Friday, 7 February.

1815 Dickens family moves to London.

1817 Dickens family moves to Chatham, Kent. CD goes to school, develops love of theatre, comic songs, long walks. Above all, as he wrote much later in *David Copperfield*:

'[Books and reading] kept alive my fancy and my hope of something beyond that time and place.'

1822 Dickens family moves to London; CD stays in Chatham to finish school term.

1823 CD moves to London; cleans boots and runs errands for his parents and their lodger. Sent to sell or pawn his family's possessions, including treasured story-books. His mother tries, but fails, to set up a school.

Begins lifelong habit of roaming around London, often at night, exploring poor, dirty, dangerous backyards and 'rookeries' (cheap, squalid, semi-derelict lodging houses). Meets vagrants, criminals, prostitutes, homeless people, abandoned children, people with mental-health problems. He pities them, but their irregular lives intrigue him and excite his imagination. Years later, bored but trying to write in picturesque, tranquil Switzerland, he complained: 'My figures [characters] seem to stagnate without crowds about them.'

1824 Aged 12, is sent by his parents to work in Warren's Blacking Warehouse, Hungerford Stairs, Central London. They can no longer afford to care for him; he has to earn money to buy his own food. Lives in lodgings.

A dreadful memory

Dickens looks back to his time at the blacking warehouse:

'No words can express the agony of my soul... I felt my early hopes of growing up to be a learned and distinguished man crushed in my breast... the sense I had of being utterly neglected and hapless... Misery it was to my young heart.'

John Forster,
The Life of Charles Dickens, 1872–1876

1824 Dickens's parents are imprisoned for debt in the Marshalsea gaol. They are released after John Dickens inherits a legacy from his mother.

RealCDickens Charles Dickens
It would do us no harm to remember oftener than we do, that vices are sometimes only virtues carried to excess! #dombey
164 years ago

Unfair advantage

When, in 1824, Fanny Dickens, Charles's oldest sister, wins the Royal Academy of Music's second prize for piano – and a silver medal – young Charles weeps, but not for joy. He wants the chance to study and learn and compete for prizes, as well. He feels ashamed working in the warehouse, where he is sometimes seated in the window by his employers, like a sideshow, so that passers-by can watch him work.

1825 John Dickens retires from Navy Pay Office (because of an 'Infection of the Urinary Organs') and receives a pension.

To his immense relief, CD leaves the blacking warehouse. At first, his mother is unwilling to send him back to school (quite reasonably, she worries that they will not have enough money; she would prefer CD to continue earning wages). But John Dickens is optimistic (and reckless). He sends CD to a London 'establishment': Wellington House Academy.

An ideal student?

At school, Dickens writes and performs plays with his classmates, reads lurid, popular 'scandal-sheets' (cheap magazines reporting crime, especially murders), produces a newspaper – and charges fellow pupils to read it (they pay with marbles) – and speaks a secret schoolboy language that the teachers cannot understand. He keeps pet mice in a hollowed-out textbook; one falls into the inkwell...

At the same time, whenever he has time alone, Dickens studies as hard as he can, eager to make up for the schooldays he has lost.

1827 Leaves school (aged 15) and starts work as a junior clerk in a solicitor's office. With other young clerks, he goes out drinking in the evenings (a favourite snack is boiled German sausages and porter, a heavy, sweetish beer). Plays practical jokes, such as dropping cherrystones out of upstairs office windows onto the hats of passers-by. Edward Blackmore, a solicitor, later remarked that the boy was 'exceedingly good-looking and clever'.

1829 CD finds the law boring, frustrating, absurd. Helped by his mother's brother, CD starts work as freelance shorthand reporter, recording proceedings of obscure, archaic courts held at Doctors' Commons, London. Spends most of his evenings at London theatres – he takes care to seek out the best actors, in the best roles – but also, as soon as he can, on his 18th birthday, gets a reader's ticket for the world-class library at the British Museum, and reads, reads, reads – mostly literature and history.

1830 Meets and falls head-over-heels in love with London banker's daughter, Maria Beadnell.

1831 Again helped by his uncle, CD writes reports of Westminster debates for The *Mirror of Parliament* newspaper. Praised as 'the best reporter in the [press] gallery'. Leaves parents' home – for ever – to live in lodgings with friend (a law student). Considers emigrating with same friend, to Guyana, South America.

1832 Considers career as an actor; he has memorised many speeches from plays. Arranges an audition at Covent Garden (a leading London theatre) – but is too ill in bed, with a bad cold and only a faint, hoarse voice, to attend.

Reports debates in Parliament for newspaper the *True Sun*. Writes advertising copy for the same paper – including jingles for the hateful, shameful Warren's Blacking. With typical overstatement, he calls it 'the pride of mankind'!

1833 Publishes first short story: 'A Dinner at Poplar Walk' in the *Monthly Magazine*.

Dickens's parents hold a lavish 21st birthday party for him (even though they are badly in debt). In his spare time, CD is now busy arranging and producing amateur theatricals. Amid much heartache, his friendship with Maria Beadnell ends.

1834 Becomes staff reporter for *The Morning Chronicle*; travels to Scotland; publishes more short stories in the *Monthly Magazine*. Raises money to help pay his father's debts and save him from prison, yet again. Meets Catherine Hogarth, daughter of music critic and newspaper editor George Hogarth, a Scot who admires Dickens's writing.

1835 CD pays more of his father's debts. John Dickens takes rooms with a washerwoman in Hampstead, and is soon, once again, trying to borrow money. Charles finds 'comfortable' lodgings for Elizabeth Dickens, and helps support her for the rest of his life.

Publishes stories and sketches in several different London papers and magazines, including the *Evening Chronicle*, edited by George Hogarth.

Engaged to Catherine Hogarth – but is too busy working as a roving reporter to spend much time in her company. He's also writing sketches and – new! – stories based on the darker side of London life. Tiredness makes him suffer from extremely painful spasms (perhaps kidney disease) in his side. He's had this problem since childhood.

Hello sailor!

One evening, Dickens decides to provide Catherine and her family with a surprise entertainment. Dressed in a sailor-suit, he leaps through an open window, whistles a lively tune, dances a hornpipe, then jumps out through the window again. A few minutes later, he appears at their front door in his everyday clothes, as if nothing unusual had happened. Fortunately, Catherine's family laugh obligingly at his prank.

1836 Has first big success as popular author: publishes *Sketches by Boz*. It is widely praised, but one writer makes a critical comment that still seems relevant today – at least to some of Dickens's readers:

> *'The fault of the book is the caricature of Cockneyism, of which there is too much…'*

John Forster, *The Examiner*, February 1836.

Who woz Boz?

Charles Dickens's youngest brother, Augustus, was born in 1827. Before he could even walk or talk, he was given a baby nickname, 'Moses'. As Augustus learned to speak, he stumblingly pronounced the name 'Boses', not 'Moses'. Big brother Charles copied 'Boses' for himself, but shortened it to 'Boz'. Peculiarly, Dickens experts do not all agree on how we should pronounce the name today: some say 'Bows', to rhyme with 'rose', but others say 'Boz' (to rhyme with 'was').

CD publishes the first monthly instalments of a rambling novel, *The Pickwick Papers*. He is asked to write the libretto for an opera. His favourite brother, Fred, aged 16, comes to live with him in his lodgings.

Aged 24, marries Catherine Hogarth. They go on honeymoon to a country cottage near Rochester, very close to CD's favourite childhood home.

Catherine's sister Mary reports that her new brother-in-law:

'is such a nice creature and so clever he is courted and made up to by all the literary gentlemen...'.

CD stops reporting for *The Morning Chronicle*, to devote himself to writing. Meets John Forster, who becomes his friend, literary advisor, and (later) biographer. Writes a phenomenal amount – newspaper articles, descriptive sketches for magazines, a play, comic songs, campaigning pamphlets – and makes plans for two more novels, and a story for children.

1837 Edits new monthly magazine *Bentley's Miscellany*. Publishes first monthly episode of *Oliver Twist*, and *The Pickwick Papers* in book format. As a sign of his growing fame, his real name, rather than 'Boz', appears on the title page of both.

'The popularity of this author is one of the most remarkable phenomena of recent times.'

Quarterly Review, 1837.

CD's first child, Charley, born. CD is grief-stricken after his wife's sister, Mary Hogarth, dies suddenly.

1838 Visits grim Yorkshire schools with illustrator 'Phiz' (Hablot Browne) on fact-finding tour. Publishes first instalment of *Nicholas Nickleby* (it contains a fierce attack on bad schools and cruel masters), also *Oliver Twist* in book format. CD's second child, Mary (Mamie), born.

1839 John Dickens embarrasses his son by secretly asking his publishers, editors and famous friends for money. Exasperated, Charles sends John and Elizabeth to live far away from London, near Exeter in Devon. They hate it there, and soon return.

Leaves *Bentley's Magazine* (after one of very many quarrels with publishers); publishes *Nicholas Nickleby* in one volume. Meets heiress and philanthropist Angela Burdett Coutts. Helps with her plans for social reform.

CD's third child, Katey, born.

1840 Edits and publishes new weekly magazine: *Master Humphrey's Clock*. It contains first episode of *The Old Curiosity Shop*.

1841 Starts new weekly serial: *Barnaby Rudge*. Late in the year, publishes it in book format along with *The Old Curiosity Shop*.

CD's fourth child, Walter, born.

1842 Visits North America with wife for 3 months. Loves the scenery, but not the politics. Leaves children in London with governess. Complains about Catherine's clumsiness; alleges that she has fallen over 743 times.

Publishes travel book *American Notes*, and first monthly instalment of *Martin Chuzzlewit*. Visits Cornwall with male friends.

1843 Wife's sister Georgina Hogarth moves into the Dickens' family home, to manage the children and the household.

CD is delighted; Georgina reminds him of her dead sister, Mary: 'So much of her spirit shines out…'

CD publishes first special seasonal story: *A Christmas Carol*.

1844 More quarrels with his publishers over money; signs deal with another firm. Moves family to live in Italy for a year. Publishes *Martin Chuzzlewit* in book form, and second seasonal story, *The Chimes*.

CD's fifth child, Francis, born.

1845 Tours Italy with wife. Climbs the volcano, Vesuvius. Returns to London, to direct 'the Amateurs' troupe of actors in Ben Jonson's play: *Every Man in His Humour*. Publishes third seasonal story: *The Cricket on the Hearth*.

CD's sixth child, Alfred, born.

1846 Briefly becomes editor of *The Daily News*; publishes travel book *Pictures from Italy*. CD and his family leave to live for several months in Switzerland, then Paris. Publishes fourth seasonal story: *The Battle of Life*.

1847 Returns from France. Acts with 'the Amateurs' theatrical company in Manchester and Liverpool. Helps set up Urania Cottage Home for Homeless Women, in London, funded by Angela Burdett Coutts. CD's seventh child, Sydney, born.

> *'Ah, Mr Dickens, it was a sad loss to the public when you took to writing.'*

Old stage-carpenter, after watching Dickens act in and direct a play.[1]

1848 On tour with amateur actors to several British cities. Publishes *Dombey and Son* in book form, also last seasonal story: *The Haunted Man*. CD's favourite sister, Fanny, dies from tuberculosis.

1849 Publishes first instalment of *David Copperfield* as monthly serial.

CD's eighth child, Henry (Harry), born. After meeting Scottish celebrity pioneer doctor James Simpson, and asking his advice,

1. Source: *Philip Collins (ed.)*, Dickens Interviews and Recollections, *1981*.

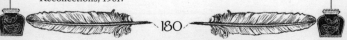

Dickens insists that Catherine be given new, controversial – and sometimes dangerous – chloroform anaesthetic to help with pain during the birth.

1850 Edits and publishes new weekly paper *Household Words*, also *David Copperfield* in book form. CD's ninth child, Dora, born.

1851 Publishes *A Child's History of England* in weekly instalments.

Directs and acts in play: *Not So Bad As We Seem* in aid of The Guild of Literature and Art (a charity that helped struggling writers and artists). Queen Victoria attends one performance.

CD's father, John Dickens, dies. CD's wife Catherine is seriously ill. Their baby, Dora, dies.

1852 Publishes *Bleak House* in monthly instalments. Performs *Not So Bad As We Seem* in UK provinces.

CD's tenth child, Edward, born.

1853 Publishes *Bleak House* in book format. Spends months with wife and children in France, then travels with male friends, novelist Wilkie Collins and painter Augustus Egg, to Switzerland and Italy.

Back in Britain, gives public readings of *A Christmas Carol*.

1854 Publishes *Hard Times* in weekly instalments in *Household Words*, then in book format. Gives more public readings in British towns and cities.

1855 Directs and acts in *The Lighthouse*, by close friend, novelist Wilkie Collins. CD meets first sweetheart Maria (née Beadnell) again; is deeply disappointed by her appearance.

Publishes *Little Dorrit* in monthly instalments. Gives many public readings. Lives in France for several months.

1856 Purchases country house, Gad's Hill Place, near Chatham.

1857 Publishes *Little Dorrit* in book format.

Gives many public readings. Directs and acts in another Wilkie Collins play: *The Frozen Deep*. Meets young actress, Nelly Ternan, a member of the cast. Son Walter leaves home to work in India.

1858 CD separates from wife; publishes personal statement about the separation in London newspaper *The Times* and in *Household Words*.

Gives many public readings for profit and for charity; tours Scotland and Ireland.

1859 Edits new weekly magazine, *All the Year Round*. Closes *Household Words*. Publishes *A Tale of Two Cities* in instalments, then in book format. Gives many more public readings.

Provides for Nelly Ternan; visits her secretly until the end of his life.

1860 Publishes *Great Expectations* in weekly instalments. CD moves to live permanently at Gad's Hill Place.

CD's daughter Katey marries; his brother Alfred dies.

Elizabeth Dickens becomes physically frail and mentally confused. Charles remains dutiful and helpful, but seems never to have forgiven his mother for failing to 'rescue' him from Warren's Blacking Warehouse.

1861 Gives a great many public readings. Publishes *Great Expectations* in book format.

CD's son Charley marries; CD does not approve.

Nelly Ternan moves to France, perhaps because she is pregnant.

1862 More public readings; several visits to France, probably to visit Nelly Ternan, who may have had Dickens's child (a son, who died) this year. CD's daughter Mamie and sister-in-law Georgina Hogarth go to live in France also.

1863 CD gives charity readings in Paris and London. Makes several visits to France.

CD's son Walter dies in India.

Elizabeth Dickens dies, aged 74. Charles comments that, towards the end, 'her condition was frightful'. His words show none of the warmth that he felt towards his father.

1864 Publishes *Our Mutual Friend* in monthly instalments. Several visits to France.

1865 Narrowly escapes death – and scandal – in railway accident while travelling back to England from France with Nelly Ternan and her mother. Publishes *Our Mutual Friend* in book format. Begins to suffer from pain and lameness in foot. CD's son Alfred leaves to settle in Australia.

1866 Public readings in several British cities.

1867 Very successful public readings in USA. But CD exhausted and increasingly unwell.

1868 Returns to UK. Problems with vision and balance after probable slight stroke, but begins triumphant 'farewell tour' of readings in UK. CD's son Edward (nicknamed 'Plorn') leaves for Australia; son Harry goes to university – his only child to receive a higher education.

1869 Breaks off 'farewell tour' because of illness.

1870 Gives last public readings in London. Publishes first instalments of *The Mystery of Edwin Drood* (it remains unfinished). Invited to meet Queen Victoria and has an audience with her at Buckingham Palace. Collapses – perhaps at Gad's Hill Place, perhaps at Nelly Ternan's house. Dies the next day (9th June).

1870 Buried at Westminster Abbey. Crowds flock to visit his tomb.

2012 The 200th anniversary of Charles Dickens's birth.[1]

1. For further details of the worldwide birthday celebrations, see www.dickens2012.org

Glossary

astrakhan Skin from unborn or newborn lambs. It has a delicate, glossy, tightly curled fleece.

blacking Boot polish, or a sticky mixture used to polish cast-iron fire-grates and stoves.

cholera An infectious disease, carried by polluted water. It caused severe diarrhoea and was often fatal.

dame school Nursery school or first school, usually run by an older woman in her own home.

dapper Exceedingly neat, smart and trim.

esquire A title used in the past to show gentlemanly status.

genteel Self-consciously, unnaturally, refined spech or manners.

gnomic Brief, obscure, mysterious.

Luddites Skilled craft-workers who rioted because they feared unemployment after new machines were invented to do their jobs, such as weaving cloth.

mesmerism A theory developed by Austrian doctor Anton Mesmer. He believed in a force called 'animal magnetism' that could be used to cure some illnesses.

pawn To hand over valuable goods in return for a short-term loan.

prison-hulks Old, worn-out sailing ships, used as floating prisons.

rakes Rich people who irresponsibly seek entertainment and pleasure.

rookeries Crowded city slums occupied by poor people.

steward Male manager, in charge of running a large household.

Index

Instant Dickens index

Throughout this book you'll find pages dedicated to the works of Charles Dickens. These snippets of 'Instant Dickens' briefly summarise the plots and themes of his works, whilst adding some background to the topics discussed therein.

Use the list below to help you to instantly discover more about Dickens's works.

Very Peculiar Histories™

Ancient Egypt
Mummy Myth and Magic
Jim Pipe
ISBN: 978-1-906714-92-5

The Blitz
David Arscott
ISBN: 978-1-907184-18-5

Brighton
David Arscott
ISBN: 978-1-906714-89-5

Castles
Jacqueline Morley
ISBN: 978-1-907184-48-2

Christmas
Fiona Macdonald
ISBN: 978-1-907184-50-5

Global Warming
Ian Graham
ISBN: 978-1-907184-51-2

Golf
David Arscott
ISBN: 978-1-907184-75-8

Great Britons
Ian Graham
ISBN: 978-1-907184-59-8

Ireland
Jim Pipe
ISBN: 978-1-905638-98-7

London
Jim Pipe
ISBN: 978-1-907184-26-0

Rations
David Arscott
ISBN: 978-1-907184-25-3

Scotland
Fiona Macdonald

Vol. 1: From ancient times
to Robert the Bruce
ISBN: 978-1-906370-91-6

Vol. 2: From the Stewarts
to modern Scotland
ISBN: 978-1-906714-79-6

The Tudors
Jim Pipe
ISBN: 978-1-907184-58-1

Vampires
Fiona Macdonald
ISBN: 978-1-907184-39-0

Victorian Servants
Fiona Macdonald
ISBN: 978-1-907184-49-9

Wales
Rupert Matthews
ISBN: 978-1-907184-19-2

Whisky
Fiona Macdonald
ISBN: 978-1-907184-76-5

William Shakespeare
Jacqueline Morley
ISBN: 978-1-908177-14-8

Yorkshire
John Malam
ISBN: 978-1-907184-57-4